My Mother's Porch

The Life Experience of A Black Gary, Indiana Girl

I0161390

Augusta Ware-DeNeal

My Mother's Porch Publishing

ISBN: 978-0-578-23955-2

PRINTED IN THE UNITED STATES OF AMERICA

The Lord says, "I will guide you along the best pathway
for your life. I will advise you and watch over you."

(Psalm 32:8)

The TRON –AGEK' Foundation, Inc. is a STEM education- oriented think tank based in Northwest, Indiana. It is a non-profit organization, designated 501(c) (3) by the IRS. It is the leading STEM education entity in the Northwest Indiana, Gary, Indiana area.

1% of the royalties of this book will be donated by the TRON/ AGEK' Foundation, Inc. to the 20th Century Missionary Baptist Church Youth Department for:

1. after-school, week-end and summer hands-on STEM initiatives for the cities of Gary, East Chicago and the Town of Merrillville for k-12 science instruction

   and

2. funding for secondary and post-secondary (TRIO-enrolled/ graduates) STEM/science mentor instructor(s) and coordinator/ clerical personnel.

Table of Contents

Part Three –
What Does Love Got to Do With It?

Introduction

My Mother's Porch is a philosophical frame of mind, a platform. In this literary piece the author shares stories regarding her life experiences growing up in the city of Gary, Indiana.

Herein lies 13 inter-relational short story narratives written by a Black girl. It is an identity and heritage given to her. It takes on a cultural lens and is staged in re-occurring running themes.

Passionately, story narratives are shared regarding the author's life experiences that include her family and early childhood, life tragedies, Sundays and church, community secondary and post-secondary personal educational views, love/youth, hometown of Gary and concludes with a final history lesson and cultural science learning recommendations (curriculum design).

Most importantly; it underscores the critical need for science/STEM training - especially in Black and Brown communities. All are told within a Black ideology and spiritual lens.

This, hopefully, is transferable and tangible work for the interested.

Research and data from the bible, recorded history and music genres are used for story narrative context and meaning. Additionally, religion has its basis in beliefs. Philosophy has its basis in reason and self-reflection.

Preface

The author uses a first person examination to express her human existence.

All well-known philosophies of education can be reduced to positions of many opinions, beliefs that become accepted scholarly writings. They are different and unique. They are supposed to be.

The author's life experience is Black. Some even say the Black experience is raw. Further, it has been suggested that we have our own language. Good point.

Therefore, she lends her voice to this rawness; because her belief is that we all need any and all platforms that contributes to the transcendence of our world to become a better place.

The question that will arise at once is "Why an attempt at another philosophical opinion or view since we have so much distinguished acceptable scholarly work already available to us?"

True.

There is an abundance of material for research and practices collected over time. However, there is still yet a need for voices that will tell the stories of the Black American experience in its "real" context regarding those constructs; most importantly spiritually.

I am not that brilliant of a person. Sometimes, I wonder if I am all that smart. However, I do know I am a determined educator, always have been. I love my community and I too believe we all have God given talents that are given to us that He uses for His purpose and design. We do not ask for the gifts and purpose given to us.

We doubt that purpose with what I call the ("Why me?" or "Couldn't you have chosen someone else?" or "I am not worthy.") questions and statements mainly because we fear what the audiences or constituencies may think of our work.

It can be risky.

But deep down inside you keep pushing to accomplish what you believe are your missions in life.

And, you perform those responsibilities in the most positive and effective way possible assured that God will provide every need - "seen" and "unseen."

So, I present this as a written discourse. It is knowledge. It is in my voice. It is to the soul of the listener. It can defend itself and it knows for whom it should speak.

Fearlessly, I present this work, unapologetic for my Christian faith.

I **pray** and **hope** that my story **informs, emboldens** and more specifically **nourishes.**

—∞—

Food For Thought

How do you know when you have been assigned a God given task? My Answer: How do you not know?

So, this is what I have done.

Welcome to **My Mother's Porch.**

(Short Story Narratives)

Dedicated to my mother, father, my boys, sisters, brothers, aunt, nieces, nephews, and cousins.

Special Dedication:

Niecy and her boys

Tron, my son

My Community

My Church

And, Ronald Collier of Chicago, Illinois (Rest in Peace baby cousin)

Part One –
'My Life' – Oh, Come and See What The Lord Has Done

Home

MY MOM AND dad were born, raised and married in the state of Mississippi and later traveled to Chicago, Illinois and finally to the city of Gary, Indiana when I was three weeks old. My family has lived in the city of Gary for more than 65 years.

My mother used to tell the story of how she was so young and excited to leave her Southern hometown with her young babies to meet her husband up North. Earlier, my father had to leave his home in the South. He left his family behind for a short period of time.

When it was time, momma took with her on the train to Chicago me, my oldest brother and three of her very young nieces. She would smile and tell us girls the story about the flat pill hat, tight-fitted flowery dress, cinnamon stockings and high-healed shoes she wore to meet my dad at the train station in Chicago. We could only imagine.

After settling up North, my parents would sometimes take all their children on the train or in my dad's car back South for summer visits. My younger brother tells the story of the old train with the large round white light on the train's front engine fast approaching the station and how amazed we would be as children of its breathtaking awesomeness and the ghostly white steam coming from underneath the train cars. We had never seen trains in real life. So, we migrated from the South to the safe havens of the far North.

Becker Street

Today, the one and only house we have ever lived in sits on Becker Street. Our family has lived there for over 50 years. It is a small white and black house surrounded by a big yard that my dad cherished in a small neighborhood of loving and life-long friends.

Our home always welcomed so many relatives and friends over the years. But the front porch is where everybody, if the weather allowed, rested. Whether the intent was to stay or not, one could easily settle into one of the comfortable seats and kick off their shoes on that porch. I have spent many hours on this porch observing mother birds feeding their baby chicks in a tall tree next to the porch window. But upon arriving and settling, you would probably end up drinking a cold iced tea my mom was so famous for; especially among her children, grandchildren and sons-in-laws.

But as you climbed the front cement stairs and upon stepping into the windowed old fashioned porch, you just felt at home. Nothing fancy, just that warm and cozy feeling. You know, like the home that reminds you of Big Ma or Auntie's house especially if you were from the south or from Gary. My mother probably would be the one who would greet you at the front door with a smile. As you entered the porch to your left, you would find beautiful house plants and other house ornaments. To the right, you'd find lawn chairs, a couch and a lawn living room table. Momma's spot however was in her rocking chair that sat in the middle of her beautiful house plants I had purchased many years earlier. Now, the chair sits empty.

On her good days, one could find momma sitting there on the porch like she was just sitting waiting for you to arrive. She always made time to listen. When she could, you could rest and be assured momma had cleaned her kitchen and the bathroom early that morning day. That was just her thing. It is funny, I inherited that same habit. I tell my niece all the time, never say you will not develop your parent's habits. You will.

So, to anyone that visited our little white and black house on Becker Street, one would find more times than not; our momma, sitting on the porch in her rocking chair. She most likely would have on one of her house dresses.

Momma always amazed me with her persona of calmness and peace.

She always had a positive word to share.

Smiling, I can picture her now.

Through My Little Eyes-
Guard Your Heart

MOMMA HAD A "unique and special love" for each one of her seven children, grandchildren, great grandchildren, nieces and nephews. I am the second oldest of seven children. She loved us. But, I was one of those smart, curious, mischievous, grown little girls. I got into trouble early in life and became pregnant at the age of 15. When I think about my childhood sometimes, I am reminded of Natalie Cole's song, "Annie Mae":

> A little girl in a great big world
> Annie Mae
> No one knew about her past
> Some people swore she'd never last
> She was growing up much too fast
> Growing
> Just a little too fast

I hurt my mom and dad when I got pregnant and spent the rest of my life trying to make up for it. When my mom thought I was feeling guilty for the hurt I had caused the family, when she felt our self-esteem needed a boost, she would say, "The past is the past. Forgive yourself. Move on. Do good." My mom and dad certainly knew how to make you feel better about yourself.

We, as children, knew what love looked like just watching them love on each other throughout our lives. The love they had for each other was genuine and is rare today, especially among the Black race. In my opinion, we have forgotten how to love, especially each other. Anyway, as a young girl, I used to wish that some day someone would love and care for me the way my dad did for my mother. Believe me he was no saint; but Sam loved his family and as far as we knew, nothing and no one came before them. Our father worked hard to provide for us. I remember him window washing, house painting and finally working in the steel mills to support us. I nicknamed my dad; *BB*. *I remember as* little children, he was the only live- in dad on the block. The neighboring kids called him *Mr. J.B.*

So, we grew up in Gary, Indiana (the most northern city in the state of Indiana) in a southern traditional home where we saw our parents together over our life time. But, the norm for us was that Black couples stayed together. That is what we saw: love between Black women and men. Whether right or wrong, married or not, we saw their commitment to each other. So, I remain faithful and hopeful in the Black couple.

I remember my mom and dad would dress up sharp and go out on the town sometimes at night. I remember them talking about the F&J Lounge. I remember also the Clayton Lounge where entertainers like Bobbie Blue Bland, Muddy Waters and B.B. King and others would perform. Momma shared with us the story of these entertainers growing up near her hometown and how one even visited my aunt in Memphis, Tennessee when he became famous. Fascinating stories.

But in preparing for the night out on the town, my dad would wave his hair with a black scarf. It would be processed, greased and cocked to the side as he and my mom exited out to their parties. Boy, my mom was so jealous of this little Black man. My mom never wore pants out to party or to church services. Instead, she wore suits and dresses like only she could wear them. My dad would tease her by saying that after several attempts, he finally caught the love of his life running through the woods of the Mississippi Delta Swamps. She never refuted the story. She only smiled at his story telling.

Later on upon their return from the night out, they would wake us up fussing like cats and dogs. We could hear them in our tiny room where all the children slept. The funny thing to us was that momma would be up early the next morning cooking. My dad's breakfast place setting would be neatly set on the table and he would be sitting there reading the daily newspaper looking just as content and happy. My mom would be cooking breakfast like nothing had happened the night before. I now know that is what you call "wed-locked." My parents were married for more than 65 years.

My dad was a provider. For me, the comedian D.L. Hughley best de-scribes the Black father's struggle. Like Hughley, my dad would work several jobs sometimes at the same time to take care of his family. However, we were complete when my dad was home, even if it was just to show us who ran stuff. I remember him taking my bedroom door off the hinges after he and I had a heated father and daughter exchange. Today, me, my sisters and brothers laugh about that one family story, among many.

I think his favorite past time was working in his beautiful yard and garden, house painting, window washing, fishing, hunting, bowl-ing, washing his car and making peanut butter brittle candy for us. But, Sam really loved to fish. He eventually could afford to purchase a used boat, which really did not get much sailing and fishing. On summer days, he would slowly drive his inherited Ford convert-ible around our Becker Street neighborhood with his cherished boat hooked up to the rear of the car. My mom would whisper to us that he was just showing off to the neighbors. Sometimes, my little neph-ew would safely ride proudly on the front seat of his grandfather's boat; without my mother's approval of course.

I remember, as a little girl, I would wonder why my dad would some-times stand back from the dinner table and watch his family eat. Later, I found out that my dad wanted to make sure that we had eat-en first and were full before he would sit down to eat his meal. Many times we only had beans and cornbread, maybe sweet cakes, maybe red Kool-Aid for a dinner meal. My mom would finally fix my dad's dinner plate. He would sit at the head of the table like he was being served steak and potatoes. We did not realize just how "po" we were.

My parents always made sure we watched the Charles Dickens play "A Christmas Carol" every Christmas together over the years. As an adult, I still do.

Christmas was and still is an all - day happy family day. One Christmas, my parents bought me a small shiny red wood desk. It was beautiful. Looking back, they must have had this desk on lay-a-way for a long time in order to have it at their house for their little girl by Christmas Day. I do remember momma putting our clothes on lay-a-way at the Robert Halls Store downtown. Anyway, I would pretend sitting at my desk that I was the school leader and my broth-ers, sisters and cousins were my students.

I always wondered how my parents knew not to buy me another White doll; but instead to purchase me a red wood grain desk with a glass sliding door on the side to store my little teacher's stuff. How did they know my passion for education at such a very young age? Books were few in our house. Looking back, we only had a big white bible where my mom kept important papers. We had a set of red and black Universal World Reference Encyclopedias. These books had the most impressionable words and pictures, I thought. I stored them on the little desk shelves and allowed my siblings to check them out by writing "due back" dates on a small piece of paper and having them sign the notes. Memories.

I do know that my parents worked hard to save up for the desk that I cherished so and other gifts to make their children happy on Christmas Day. On that day, momma would have cooked the most gracious Christmas dinner we could afford that year. We would have a beautiful green decorated Christmas tree that we would have purchased from the fruit and vegetable market which was located across the railroad train tracks on Broadway Street. Our tree would always stand at the living room window of our apartments with blinking lights. As children, we were always so proud of our Christmas trees over the years. Also, my mom would have a big candy and fruit dish on the living room cocktail table.

We looked forward to the homemade grits or rice and bread that would be ready before school. Our little brown lunch school bag usually held a peanut butter and jelly or bologna sandwich. When we were lucky, a surplus canned meat sandwich would be in our little brown paper bags instead of the former. Dinner would be prepared when we got home from school. It was always good to us. Many times, I have purchased food at the local A&P Grocery Store with a $65 book of food stamps that my parents sometimes would barter with others in the neighborhood to receive more food than the price of the food stamps. You know what I mean. Don't play!

After school, we ate our dinner, did our homework, watched either cartoons, Bozo Show, He Haw, the Lucy Show or Mr. Ed, Cowboy movies, Ed Sullivan Show or Garfield Goose and Friends and went to bed. My youngest brother recalls when we got our first color television set after my parents received their long awaited income tax check one year. We were so proud. All of our friends would come over and watch television with us. We eventually got a telephone and maintained the same telephone number for over 40 years (XXX-6861) until we disconnected it after my mom's transition. Did that hurt.

My dad loved listening to spirituals and watching biblical stories on television, mostly on Sunday mornings. His family never owned a television and we never saw one while visiting the south during the summers. He would rise early on Sunday mornings, open the windows and turn on the Gospel Jubilee Showcase Singing Show on our first black and white TV. As children, we used to laugh at him. I look forward to watching old biblical movies during the holidays like *The Bible, The Robe,* and *The Ten Commandments.* I really loved the story of *Saint Bernadette of Lourdes.* I continue to watch these movies.

I always feel like my dad is watching them with me. He passed at the young age of 59, way too early.

Some of my earlier memories were when we as small children stayed in two-bedroom apartments before moving to Becker Street. Growing up people always referred to our apartment community as the "Border" in the Froebel School District area.

Some would say this was one of the rough sides of Gary. If it was, we did not know it. To us, it was home; our community. Mostly everybody knew each other in the neighborhood or district. My brothers had their own little gangs (Purple Gang) where they competed by playing basketball or baseball against each other. Occasionally, a fight would break out. The very next day or shortly thereafter, we would end up hanging out with each other, playing kickball, dodge, tag, jumping rope, playing pitty-pat or eating together at one of our houses.

If my Aunt Sarah, Ms. Lee or especially Ms. Feagon (our community bible teacher) told on you for misbehaving, that was a sure a** "whipping." My mom was left-handed and she could whip butt with that left hand; especially with a tree switch that she allowed you to go out and select first. By chance, if you selected a switch that did not meet her satisfaction, she would in return go out and get her own.

I remember how we would play outside in front of our apartment building after school. It was law that we be in the house when the street lights came on. While playing outside at night, we could smell the Greek neighborhood bakery baking goods for their next day's business. Sometimes, if we had some change, we would stop and buy a glazed doughnut and maybe a carton of chocolate milk before school the next day.

After school and on weekends, we would play skip rope or play Tag with our mothers sitting outside with us laughing, sharing the neighborhood gossip and exchanging policy numbers. Young readers, policy was our lottery back then. My mother had a *Green Book* that she used to select her numbers e.g., the numbers 123 played for clear water etc. The policy lady, Ms. Sally, would pick up my mother's numbers, give her a receipt or she would go to the policy house to play her numbers. Sometimes my mom would take us with her. If you hit or if you won, the policy man or woman would bring your winnings to your house. It always amazed me that all the policy workers knew each community member's daily numbers they played at their local policy house! My aunt had her own policy house for a while and I remember riding around with my uncle to pick up and pass out the winnings! My uncle would be dressed to kill. He would always wear shiny pointed toe shoes.

Voting was very important to our parents and community. Remember Blacks had only been allowed to vote since 1965. So, it was not until after me and my brother's birth did my parents have this new freedom right to vote. They had seen a lot growing up in the South. They knew how important it was to cast their ballots. To my knowledge, neither of my parents missed voting. They always reminded us to vote when we became of age. It is so important that our young people of color not only unite but more importantly, vote. My parents would dress in their Sunday best and travel to the voting spots for our neighborhood where other neighbors would gather and mostly discuss the election day.

As a young child, I did not quite understand the power of the Black vote or the negative forces behind voting suppression. It is so important that our children understand why it is so critical for our race to continue to vote and to protect the voting rights for which the battle continues today. We have to remind them continuously because people of color cannot afford to stay away from the voting polls. Stacy Abrams (2020) reminds us that this is a serious time for our country. It is as serious as it was before the Voting Rights Act of 1965 when Blacks could not vote. It is as serious as the legislation gutting out the Voting Rights Act as recent as 2018. It is a serious and strange time where Blacks and other people of color, renters, poor, immigrants are being excluded in our present-day census count thus attempting to eliminate rights and underfunding of designated populations from receiving federal funding. Even more serious is the fact that the current census process tabulations will be done mostly on line while most underserved populations do not have access to the Internet. It is as serious as the government re-drawing territorial lines that scatter citizenry votes (gerrymandering).

The last year of my mom's life, my sister rolled her in a wheelchair to the neighborhood voting spot where she cast her last vote. She was determined. Memories.

—∞—

Food For Thought

Vote!

Vote so that we will have the resources and political power to not only receive what the community needs but what it desires like good stable jobs, good schools, healthy neighborhoods and politicians that demonstrate they care and not just by their spoken words.

Our Way – There Is No Place Like Home

MOM AND DAD cherished their moments together. We as children could tell. I remember how my mother always kept their room neat with beautiful quilts given to her by my grandparents or spreads from the Salvation Army.

Sometimes, my mom washed, greased my dad's hair with Sulfur-Eight or the grease in the red can and sometimes dyed his hair (always black). They both would talk and laugh among themselves during their many shared moments.

Growing up in our house, our parents and big brothers (T and step-brother Sonny) used to play records by Sam Cooke, Aretha Franklin, Otis Redding, James Brown, Nina Simone, B.B. King, Muddy Waters and others which all are voices seeking or forgiving love. As children, we would sneak in the basement and listen to my oldest brother's music. Even trash talking comedian Moms Mabley's records, with her adulterated lyrics, spoke on Black love. Her comedy lyrics demonstrates Black rawness.

Today, the media tell us no lasting love exists between a Black woman and man. Artists like Angie Stone tell us different.

> Oh oh oh oh oh oh
> Ooh girl
> He is my king (she is my woman)
> Black brother, I love you
> ---------- "Brotha"

Looking at today's world, we were so blessed to have grown up in this normalcy. I am so glad me and my brothers, sisters and grandchildren saw, experienced and shared these memorable experiences with my parents.

Several times, I saw our mom washing clothes by hand (sometimes using a scrub board) when laundromat money was low in our house. She would hang them inside or outside to dry. Our new house was sold to my parents with a used washer and dryer. We were in heaven. We knew we had finally arrived. My dad never wanted my mom to work. She was always at home when she was not in the hospital or visiting her family in Chicago, Memphis or Mississippi. Momma was sick all of her life; especially her adulthood and my childhood of which has been one of the worst pains in our lives. During these times, as the oldest girl, I bore the responsibility along with my dad of taking care of my brothers and sisters. All I knew was to take care of my siblings.

My Grandma C, my mother's mother, would come up North to stay with us when my mother was very ill or hospitalized for as long as she could before she became ill herself. Grandma C taught me how to cook greens and cornbread when I was 10 years old. We learned so many life-long lessons when my grandma stayed with us and when we visited her downsouth. She taught us about life. The passed down wisdom of a grandmother is a gift. There was always enough love, wisdom and sharing from Grandma C for all of us to remember and cling to.

I remember her old tin house papered in newspaper on the inside walls. Her house sat back on a red dirt road in Long Hill, Mississippi. One could open the front door and see clear through the house back door at the dirt road leading to our cousin's farm land and the pond in our pasture. Like any farm at that time, there were a few pigs, cows, a horse or two, vegetable gardens, a sweet potato cave and a huge pecan tree where all the children played. In her aluminum tin roofed house sat a large black iron wrought bed where I and so many other children were delivered by a midwife my mom often referred to as Ms. Addie. When I purchased my birth certificate as an adult, it read *"born-a colored girl."* There were pictures of Jesus, Martin Luther King and President John Kennedy on the living room walls. Chickens and a rooster or two would be running around the house pecking the ground. We had an outside smoke house where my grandfather would store pork meat to be salted over a period of time.

My grandma would make *crackling* and *hog head souse.* She always stored peanuts. We looked forward to her northern visits or another family member bringing my grandma's homemade food back home to us. I remember looking down through some nailed down wood floor planks seeing grass growing underneath my grandma's house. She had a huge vegetable garden on the red dirt hill alongside her and Ms. Sarah's house where we would run and play for hours at a time. The cows, mule and horse would be in the pasture surrounding the house. Childhood memories. There were pear trees in the front where my grandma would pick to make preserves. She stored them on her kitchen wall shelf along with the jars of pickled pickles, pickled beets, onion and tomatoes, fig preserves and her wonderful vegetable Chow-Chow. I used to wonder why she referred to this process as canning when the picked fruits and vegetables were stored in Mason jars! I remember the homemade buttermilk biscuits, homemade butter and homemade sugar syrup she would make for us. Memories.

My grandma was a Morning Star member and active in her Southern community. She was a well-spoken, religious woman. My grandfather was known for his quiet, no-nonsense character in our little southern town. When he spoke, everybody listened.

There was no color décor or nothing matched in my grandmother's house. A big green refrigerator sat in her kitchen next to the cast iron pot and pans. There sat also a churn for milk and butter. There was a big black pot that my grandfather heated that sat in the front of the house where my grandma made soap and washed our clothes.

I remember we did not have an inside bathroom or running water. Our duty as kids was to walk down to the water spring and "fetch" water in the water buckets. I was always afraid a snake would bite me. It never did. We had a bathroom outhouse across the road that I hated using because the chickens would frequent sometimes and I was always running from the big roosters! I remember going to the Long Hill Missionary Baptist Church that had a cemetery alongside of the building. There was a pond in back of the church where I saw my oldest brother get baptized. There were some horses and cows drinking water on the other side of the pond; all on a bright and beautiful Mississippi day. All the elder church women wore pure white and everybody sang:

Wade in the water
Wade in the water children
Wade in the water
God's gonna trouble the water
Who's that young girl dressed in red
Wade in the water
Must be the children that Moses led
God's gonna trouble the water

Eva Cassidy

We would have traveled to our Mississippi "*toe-tapping, tambourine shaking*" church in either my grandfather's shiny old black car or in his horse driven buggy. The church and cemetery still exist today.

I remember picking cotton for a small salary and eating a lunch of Colby cheese and vanilla wafers under shades of big pine trees. I loved the smell of pine. It was fun to me. However, this was how my grandparents mostly made their living. My grandparents would allow us to spend some of our little earnings to purchase cookies and candy from the rolling store that would expectedly pass through our little town every now and then.

I remember when the pastor would be our guest for dinner after church. We hated those Sundays because the children always ate after the pastor and other guests had been served. It seemed like we waited forever to eat. One time to my surprise, I found out that the chickens that I had played with earlier were included in the delicious dinner meal that day. I remember chasing my younger sister around and under my grandma's house with bugs.

Vividly, deeply rooted memories remain with me as an adult.

I used to wonder why my dad never stopped other than for us to get gas or use the washrooms as we traveled north and south on the highways for family visits and funerals. We would always have packed food of fried chicken, bread, cake, juice and blankets to cover up with at night for our trips. Now, I know, this was my dad's way of protecting us because in the early 50s and 60s; highway roads were not really safe for people of color to travel. When we traveled to *Town*, I was always struck by the bathrooms and water fountain signs that read "For Coloreds Only" and "For Whites Only." It always made me fear as a child.

Also, I remember helping my grandma prepare foods to be sold at the annual picnic. Everybody would come from afar for the wonderful food and activities. Well this particular summer, a White family walked up to our food table display to purchase some delicacies. I heard my grandma say, "Yes Ma'am" and "No Ma'am" to these two little girls from this family. This disturbed me. Our parents and grandparents always taught us to be respectful and to respect and say this to adults.

So, later on that night, I asked my grandma, "Why did you say, Yes Ma'am and No Ma'am to those little children and their parents today?" She responded, "When you get older, you will understand." Unbeknownst to me, her concern was to feed her family and grandchildren that summer. So, it was then that I started to understand *"the struggle"* that is referred to at home, on the streets and in our different cultural juandras. That was the last time we stayed at my grandma's house and the last time I saw her alive.

But, on our last summer visit South as children, I remember one day sitting on a hill in front of the house longing to go back home to the North, just praying. Suddenly, I heard the sound of a car coming and then this blue car turned down the road and passed Ms. Sarah's house traveling to our house. I recognized my dad. He was coming to take me, my little sister and two brothers back home. I could not wait to see my mom and to tell her what had went on that summer at Grandma C's house. Momma loved my stories.

Back home, I remember braiding my two little sister's hair (they tease me about that today) and making sure all my siblings were properly dressed for church, school and school functions when my mom was too sick and could not herself. Many of our school and church starched and iron clothes also came from the Salvation Army. We wore them proudly. I remember one of my cousins gave me their old "Jacqueline" shoes in elementary school. These were the shoes that all the girls were wearing, I thought, anyway.

Anybody that wore them had status in elementary school.

I always wanted a pair but never bothered my parents about it. They had enough to worry about. However, my "hand-me-down" shoes had a hole in the bottom of the right shoe and I patched that hole with a cardboard box piece. I patched and polished them at night and wore them as long as I could. I remember my father working all the time and attending to my mom's illnesses. So, we continued as a family. What else were we supposed to do?

Never shall I forget the day the hospital nurses pushed my mom into a small room in anticipation of her passing because she was so very ill. I was 16 and pregnant, my oldest brother had just been shot in the back and had been paralyzed. All I could think about was how my brother and I had hurt such a beautiful mother and father. Momma pulled through that time and we took her back home. We witnessed her pulling through so many illnesses in our life time.

Almost every day, my mom would ask us if we had homework after school and would make us do it or so she thought. She would even make us pull out the old red and black encyclopedias. If we said we did not have homework, momma would make us read a school book or newspaper or so she thought. For you see, my parents had an elementary education. But, one really would not know it. But, I knew and that always hurt me. It always pained me to hear momma talk about how in the South they would hit her left hand when she would try to write with it instead of her right hand. In my opinion, that traumatized her as a child. My dad only had an eighth-grade education. But, because of their faith, survival wisdom and common sense, the family survived.

We, as children and adults, always assisted my parents with completing or reading important business documents. They both pretended a lot; but all of us knew. I always wanted to be married like my mom. It broke my heart when in her last days she woke up and said to me "You always admired my wedding rings….." and gave them to me. I wear part of the ring set today.

My mom would tell us how she wished she had the educational opportunities we had today. She would tell us girls that it was alright to marry. She wanted us to marry and be happy. But, she also would encourage us to get our college education by saying to us - "Just in case; Just in case things do not fall in place." I am so glad we listened. I am so glad I finally listened.

Most importantly, my mom loved the Lord and gave us a Christian foundation. I refer to it as a spiritual development foundation. We went to Sunday and evening services. We attended Bible Study, Sunday School and Choir Rehearsals, etc. There was a family rule - no church service that week; no after school play functions during the week. My dad was a deacon at our church. He would sit up in front of the church with the other deacons with a suit and tie on and white steel mill socks! We would be so embarrassed. When we got on him about it, he would say, "I am not thinking about what people say. I am not here for them."

I am so honored that his name is engraved on the cornerstone of our historical church building along with other founding deacons. My prayer is that we reclaim the importance of the father in the Black family in order to help give them their dignity back as they lead us again. Most importantly, fathers must understand how important they are to the family. They are the head and not the tail. As an educator of color, we have let generations of our children of color down when so many are fatherless, fostered, jailed, killed or under unemployed. Someone said, "A child without a father is like a house without a roof." No doubt there are exceptions to this abnormality. But, for many communities, this has become the norm.

In conclusion and Food For Thought: my parents and grandparents had beautiful unselfish spirits. They had beautiful hearts. Occasionally, momma would talk about guarding your heart and would remind us of a bible verse:

"Above all else, guard your heart, for everything you do flows from it." Proverbs 4:23

STORY **Four**

Tron

I GOT UP early one morning like I normally do in retirement and turned on the television and there was a documentary on about Biggie Smalls, the musician. Biggie's mom was giving an interview about her and her son's relationship. She mentioned that Biggie finally called after several days of not hearing from him. His mother stated that she had no idea of what part of the world her son was visiting or touring at that time. Upon finally hearing his voice, she told Biggie that she was mad at him for not sharing his whereabouts with her. Biggie said to her, "You owe me an apology and say you love me." I am paraphrasing here. And, he further went on to say to his mother, "I will not hang up, until you do."

His mom hung up. After an hour or two, she picked the phone up to call somebody and Biggie was still on the phone. She said, "Hello." Biggie said," Mom, I have been to sleep waiting for you to return to the phone." He said, "Mom, I am waiting." She said in final return, "Ok, I am sorry and I love you." They both hung up. I thought out of all the things she could have said about Biggie in the interview; she was telling the story of some last times spent with her child. This time, it was the message of saying "I Love You" to probably what would be one of the last times she would get that chance.

I did not tell my child how much I loved him the last time I saw him. But he knew it. The last time I saw Antron (Tron) alive, I warned him about the boys that were about to pick him up that evening. Later on, that would prove to be true.

The last time I saw Tron was on my mother's porch. He was looking out the right front window, next to the flowers, waiting for his friends to pick him up. I told him that the boys he was hanging out with were not his friends and that they would get him in trouble and "leave him" one day. I have thought about that day so many times over these past 33 years. That is exactly what happened to him.

Sure enough, the next time we heard, the police officials could not identify a Black teen's body that appeared to be 16 years old. The coroners had labeled my baby's body a "John Doe." For a day and night, we could not find him. He laid there by himself. He died alone. All the other boys ran away. They left him lying there.

When I finally got up the nerves to call the Coroners Office after hearing about a young male teen body they had picked up from the city, the coroner asked me in return if there were any identifiable marks on my child's body. When Tron was a little boy, my dad parked his used motorcycle in front of the house for a short minute. We looked away only for a second and this little inquisitive boy tried to climb on the hot motorcycle bike pipe and burned his right thigh. I asked the coroner if the body had that type of burnt mark? He answered, "Yes."

Not knowing the location of your child; especially after an unusual period of time is the most terrible feeling in the world; that gut wrenching feeling. As a Black mother, I always tried to prepare my son for the streets, especially the streets of Gary. I told Tron if he ever got in trouble and I was not around to help him, focus on me and say "Lord, have mercy." I believe he did when that bullet struck the back of his head. We, believe, the man who shot him from his porch from across the street, was a marksman. His intent was to kill. So, I wanted to face the shooter to simply ask him, Why? Why, my child? Did it mean that much to your mentality to shoot to kill? Did that car mean that much to you? I wanted to face him alone. The Lord answered my prayer.

The very next day, I drove to the blood stained spot where my son had lain and a man was coming out of the building above it. I knew it was him. So, I asked him if Brooke was his last name? He responded, "Yes." I asked, "Do you believe in God?" He responded, "Yes." Then I asked, "Why did you kill my child?" He backed away from me like he was looking at a ghost, got in his car and drove off. The next time I saw him would be in the courtroom and many times thereafter as continuous *overshadowing ghosts* in my day visions and night dreams for the rest of my life.

Tron's father and my brother had to identify my son's body so officials could remove the missing person's title of "John Doe" from his body. I remember hearing while at the funeral home the clanking of what sounded like kitchen pots and pans, no doubt funeral equipment. My family still cannot hold a conversation about Tron.

When someone called me from my mother's house to tell me about Tron not coming home to my mom's house that night and after we called the police, and other places, a strange sharp pain hit my heart about midnight the night of his death. I remember looking out my window and seeing a beautiful full moon.

Every time I hear the song, Cajun Moon:

> Cajun moon, where does your power lie
> As you move across the southern sky
> You took my bab[y] way too soon
> What have you done. Cajun moon.....

I think of that night.

But, I was saying to myself that he was a growing maturing teen. And, this probably was his first time staying out all night. At the same time, praying that he would walk in the door and I would get the phone call that he was safe at momma's house.

Birds always sang during the day around my house. But, when I walked out of my front door the next morning headed to my mom's house; it seemed like they had stopped singing, no noise at all in that time and place. Looking back, the angels had already ushered Tron to heaven. He knew the Lord. He was only a child, a baby. *I had Tron when I was 16 years old and the Lord took him at 16 years of age. The worst pain in my life.* He was such a joy to us. My first born, my first boy and my parent's first grandchild.

Samantha, my best friend slept with me the next night after hearing the painful news of Tron's death at my mom's house in his bedroom. She rocked me like a baby as I cried in her arms because I could not understand my child dying like that. None of us could. Children are not supposed to die this way. They are not supposed to die before their parents. That was a long time ago and I still do not understand. What I do know is a piece of my *heart* was ripped away. Passing time, faith, prayer, my church, a loving family, my friends and students strengthens my life. I am so very grateful. After all these many years,

I feel, it is wonderful God saw fit to even give me the words and strength to minister and counsel using the "Tron" story. His plan.

But, this only occurs when I really, really have no other option of words or deeds to encourage them. These are times when I know deep down inside they need to be comforted by me the most.

It can be hard sometimes.

Tron called my mother Momma and nicknamed me "Joy." My parents took care of him while I finished high school and worked part-time after school and on weekends. A true blessing. Most young girls are not as fortunate. For you see, once you have children, they become your responsibility for the rest of your life; your world, your joy and your pain. There is nothing smart or cute about assuming responsibilities that you know you should not for whatever reason at an early, cherished age. Surely, your whole life changes after that. You really do become an adult for the rest of your life.

I was blessed because I had parents that helped me raise my son. They wanted me to finish high school so I could provide for me and my child. When I look at the young girls today surviving with kids fatherless, on their own, my heart goes out to them. Man, I hurt my parents and siblings when I got pregnant. Again, momma would tell me when she thought I needed to be reminded every now and then that "everybody makes mistakes in life."

Nevertheless, I do still wonder if the shooter had another chance to tell the truth about what happened, would he? If I could, I would ask him, did you really find a gun by my son's hand as you mentioned in your first trial that ended up in a hung jury? Who are you? If you could recall that night, would you have come out of the house with the intention of killing? Do your kids know what you did? My three boys certainly have had too. They have grown up with little or no memory of their oldest brother. They learned early in their youth about the direct feeling of pain as it is in so many Black families affected by the killing of children. How could my children not feel pain? I tried to shelter them, my nephews and nieces, cousins from my pain all my life.

The shooter was finally charged after going to court a total of three times. He could have told the truth, even at the civil trial. Instead, his lawyers doubled down on a child thus proving that he was a criminal. Lord Have Mercy. They even convinced the court that they found a gun by my son's hands. Who will ever know? Out of all these years, I still do not know what really happened, probably never will until I get to heaven.

After we buried Tron, he came to me in a dream and flew me around the place where it happened and said to me, "I told you Joy, I did not do it." Tron had no criminal record. His autopsy showed him a healthy teen male body with no drugs in his system. It hurt so bad when I cleaned out his school locker.

Tron had just been asked to play on his high school basketball team as a start-up player. That was his dream. He could play basketball too. As a little boy, he played on different city basketball teams. He won trophies and certificates. He had a quiet spirit about himself and a smile that would melt any girl's heart; including mine. I asked him one day who his favorite basketball player was and he responded, "Larry Bird."

The black blood stain where he had lain; still remains, even after all these years on Sullivan Street. Years later, my brother told me he and my father tried to clean all the blood up. But, some still remains today. I drive down the street occasionally. As a matter of fact, this street is now alongside the elementary school that I loved growing up in my neighborhood. Today, the area is a park. I find it so ironic that this place of death for so long is now surrounded by the beauty of flowers and trees.

When my mother was passing, a few friends and family names she would whisper or call out. People say when you are making your transition from earth to heaven, you see your entire life flash before your eyes. My mother called out every member of our little family, except for Tron. She pained throughout her life over her first grandchild's death. Just the way he had to die, I think, bothered all of us the most.

One morning we all were gathered in the kitchen before we buried Tron. BB was sitting in his chair, only slightly taking his eyes off my mom. Out of nowhere, momma said in a soft gentle voice, "Whoever shot my baby down on the streets, knew exactly what he was doing." The kitchen chatter was silenced. The kitchen became dark at that moment. I never heard her straight out mention Tron or the shooter first in any conversation over the years. She only listened to me.

So, the wealthy man that shot my son was tried three times. He stuck to his story; one that he has had to live with the rest of his life. He had status in the city and his money talked. The legal team he hired was nationally well-known. They did their job. My young public defender worked his heart out. Just like us, he was outwardly shaken by the judge's reading of the final second verdict. He tried so hard to prove his case. The shooter's lawyers were successful. During the trials, I would sit in the courtroom, staring and listening to this man and his lawyers berate my son while at the same time wondering if they had a heart for children at all. I would take my college homework with me. The first trial was a hung jury. At the second trial they would not let me sit in the court room, only for the verdict. I remember the judge reading the final verdict and saying, "I wish I had tried this case." The verdict was read *"Not guilty."* We all walked away and would experience an *unspeakable* hurt that only God could begin to mend over a lifetime, if there is such a thing. I will never ever forget my baby brother's face (his best friend and uncle) when I told him that Tron was no longer with us and how it happened. Devastating.

> When the day came for the heavenly beings to appear before the Lord.
>
> Satan was there among them. The Lord asked him, "What have you been doing?"
>
> Satan answered, I have been walking here and there, roaming around the earth."
>
> (Good News Bible, Job 1:6-7).

March 22, 1986, the night of Tron's death was no different.

My baby brother told me he saw my life completely change right before his eyes after that day.

The shooter was found *Guilty* in the third trail, a civil trial. We were instructed to sue. In return for the shooter's actions, we received a $2,000 check years later. I will never ever forget the young Black lawyer we hired for the civil case. She brought the check and court release papers to my house. She explained to my three little boys what had happened and how not to be caught up in a situation like their brother; how much pain this had caused. I remember the look on their faces as she spoke. So, whether I talked about or showed any sign of grief, my children lived this life with me. The shooter disappeared to another state.

Interesting, I was on my way to church this morning and decided to stop to get a Sunday newspaper first. This was very unusual for me on a Sunday morning. Anyway, I was having trouble hooking the back of my dress. So, I decided to ask the first lady I saw to hook it for me. Uncomfortably, it was catching the back of my hair roll that I had gelled down into what I call my "Do-Do" on a bad hair day.

There was this young woman standing at the front door as I walked into my local gas station. I asked her to hook my dress. She did and at the same time she asked me if I was going to church? I answered, "Yes." She said, "Pray for me. My son was killed in Chicago four days ago and I am about to bury him in a few days." I felt those same pains I felt on March 22, 33 years ago when my son was killed. My heart dropped. We stood in the middle of the gas station's floor hugging and crying. I told her about my son and ministered to her. She told me her name. "Renay," she said.

So, I am praying for all the Renays from Chicago and around our country that are burying their murdered children today, tomorrow and in the future if we do not stop the gun violence. There are so many of us.

Thus far this year, so many people have fallen victim to homicides (mostly gun related) in our city, the Steel City (Gary, Indiana). More than twice as many people (64) have been wounded by gunfire in 2019 (only halfway through the year), Gary police show. The number stood at 71 in 2018. All of this is reported by the Post Tribune, 2019. This same article asks where is the outrage? Where is the reeling? It goes on further to ask, have we become so accustomed to mass shooting events? It states that, "Too many folks in the region have become calloused to news of shootings and homicides in Gary. It further goes on to say, that what's happening in Gary is no less a threat to our community fabric than the threat of mass shootings."

All too often, gunfire on city streets claims innocent victims, often when they weren't the intended targets. Ignoring or not giving attention to a problem, just because "that's just what always happens in Gary," is not a tenable response (Post Tribune, 2019). A young boy was killed in my city just yesterday by a police officer. Why kill? I ask again, why not maim, if you have to shoot somebody? Another was gunned down in a neighboring city as he walked to his mother's car to get some money change out if it. A seven- year- old was shot by a drive by shooting on Christmas Day yesterday.

At this time, 29 or more Americans were gunned down in the streets of our country. After 20 children were gunned down in Sandy Hook, nothing happened. After 58 were killed at an outdoor concert in Las Vegas, nothing happened. There have been over 780 Anti-Semantic attacks in our country since January, 2019. So much hatred and mental illness.

There have been 250 mass shootings in America since January 1, 2019 (Post Tribune, 2019). American police have killed 5,000 American citizens compared to the country of England's three! (RT News, 2019). "Black men, unarmed black teenagers, unharmed Black children are being killed at an alarming, frightening level as we speak."

The LaQuan McDonald case where a young Black man was shot 16 times by a police officer is very painful. As we now know, the police officer, the shooter, received a short jail sentence. The law needs to be changed that protect policeman that are shielded from the legal process that embodies Jim Crow laws that allow short prison sentences for police officers. Recently, a young Black woman, in the prime of her life was shot down in her family's residence by a police officer that was new on the force and never announced himself as a police officer at the scene of the crime.

There are so many Black youth and men being shot down on the streets of Lawndale in Chicago, Illinois. It hurts.

So, it does not matter who or where you are, how much education you have, whether you have a criminal record; there is a chance you will be shot if you live in a Black or Brown neighborhood until somebody tells me different.

But the biggest hurt is when innocent children cannot come out of their houses for fear of being shot down. Recently, a little 7-year-old girl was shot trick-a-treating and a 13-year-old was shot two times in her stomach. When the media asked what she wanted to say to the shooters, she simply and softly stated, "Put the guns down." I ask, is anybody listening?

Our country has a gun problem!!!

Get rid of the guns; assault weapons. Revamp Stand Your Ground Laws. There are more guns in the U.S. than people (NEWSY, 2019).

I repeat, get rid of the guns! My son was killed with a Smith and Wesson gun the autopsy showed.

I have not put the tombstone on Tron's grave yet for some reason after all these many years.

---∞---

Food For Thought

We have to trust God; even if we cannot trace Him.

You reap what you sow.

Chris Rock at a comedy setting stated and I paraphrase "If you want to do something about our country's gun problem? My solution is charge $5,000.00 for each bullet."

"J" - Is His Name

A FEW YEARS after Tron's death, still so full of pain, I found myself driving around Lake Michigan, the beautiful waterfront section of Gary searching for some relief from the sharp pain I was carrying in my heart. Looking at large bodies of water gives me comfort. I really was contemplating suicide. I admit, in my insanity of my child's horrible death, I even drove around the shooter's house with a gun thinking of all the bad things I wanted to happen to the man who shot my son. As I look back, what an insane thing to do. Hell, I was insane!

But, as I started to drive around the lake front, I clearly heard a voice say, "You have got to live for J." The voice continued to say, "Trust God."

"J" is his nickname; Tron's baby brother.

I thought about how Tron loved his little brothers, J and Hakim. Isaac, his youngest brother (his twin) was yet to be born.

J had been diagnosed with leukemia before Tron's death and was not supposed to live past three years of age. As I think about it, Tron would play so rough with his little brother knowing he was sick sometimes. I would fuss all the time. What I would have never imagined was that Tron was getting him ready for the battle of his life – cancer. Tron lived to watch his baby brother fight for his life and win. J even went on a Disney World trip sponsored by a major Chicago hospital (University of Chicago – Wyler's) and Make- A-Wish foundation for children with chronic illnesses with expected short life spans. Hospital officials did not expect this child to live.

When we first took J to this Chicago hospital, they found a black mass of tumor covering his chest. After three days, the doctors x-rayed his little body again. While waiting in the lobby for the doctor to share the results, I saw the doctors looking puzzled at each other. They shared with me in disbelief that the tumor was gone even before major treatment.

J had the best doctors and hospital care and was put on a regimen of medicine designed by Great Britain and tested on a sample of American children 36 years ago. He received chemotherapy, radiation, many medicines and Chicago hospital stays. I remember one day while J was asleep, I found an empty hospital room. I needed to talk to God. Boldly, I stood before Him. And, I simply asked the Lord "*not to leave us through this crisis.*" He did not. He sent an angel. We shall never forget J's main doctor, Dr. James Buckman, our angel. He was a gifted doctor in his youth cancer oncology field. He guided my child's medical protocol and recovery for over three years. He was indeed an expert in his oncology medical field. I *will always remember him making the nurses rinse J's mouth out with hydrogen peroxide all the time.*

After hearing the voice reminding me to trust God, I really realized other kids had died who were treated with the same new medicines and one on the plane to Disney but; not, J. I found an inner strength to go on with my life. J lives today. Today, he is in his early forties and truly a mother's boy.

God blessed me with another amazing Black baby boy two years before Tron's heavenly transition. He is a very talented, left-handed author, musician and writer with a pastoral heart. Tron loved music and would take this baby boy to his bedroom for hours with the music up loud. I fussed about it but, I now know that he was getting his baby brother prepared for his life-long love of music. I always noticed this child's musical talents. I always blamed myself for not embracing what he really wanted to do in life more while he was growing up. I hope and pray some artist will notice this God given, school and church drummer's talents as he pursues his musical dream. I could never persuade him to focus on other educational opportunities and still cannot. So, I stop trying and just support Hakim as he needs me. Today, he is employed in a field that he truly enjoys: construction. My left-handed son continues to write and record.

I gave birth to a baby boy two years after Tron's death, my passionate writer, Isaac. I wish Tron could have met his baby brother. They are so much alike, my protectors. Isaac, my youngest son recently got an article and book published and now has found his niche working in the IT business and authorship. Thank God!

All three of my boys love the Lord and have their own individual talents and gentlemen ways. This is by far one of the greatest gifts a mother can receive. *Thank you Jesus.*

Yes, my heart goes back to that night when I saw Tron on my mother's porch; but it also reminds me of the love and, bond between a boy, his siblings and his mother – *unconditional and unbreakable.* My boys have been the joy of my life and they let me know I am theirs. They will do just fine in life.

Today when they come home for the holidays or for a visit, I cook, wash, love on them and send them back out in the world.

Their father said to me one time when we were worrying about an issue one of them had, "Joy, our boys are men now. All you can do is provide a home for them when they need it." He was right. However, I still keep my eye on J. He lives on his own with PTSD after his military experience. He received a dishonorable discharge for smoking marijuana the last few months before his time ended with the service. Now, over 15 years later, weed is legal over many states. Yet, the military refuses to give him military benefits! But; God continues to provide for him.

Tron's death and J's illness changed my life forever. I could never look at life the same.

—⊶✕⊷—

Food For Thought

I had to surrender and Trust God.

Forgiveness

ON THE SUBJECT of forgiveness, God forgives me. Who am I not to forgive? We all have abased and abounded (hurt and been hurt). I try to forgive because I have seen what un-forgiveness does to a person. I did not say I will not forget. I had a good counselor Sista tell me "writing" helped me breathe throughout life. True, it has been the one work skill set that supported my long career in higher education while serving in Gary, Indiana.

But on the subject of forgiveness, I find "self" forgiveness as the most difficult and actually the hardest starting point of the forgiveness process for me because the bible says we are always working against ourselves.

Apostle Paul teaches us this way: "for I do not do the good I want to do, but the evil I do not want to do" (Romans 7:19). I believe God is most glorified when we are most satisfied "in" Him through forgiveness. I used to wonder what the thorn was in Apostle Paul's side as spoken of in the bible. I always thought it was the killing and mistreatment of the Gentile people. Recent research revealed that he was tormented with a spirit of his murdering of a young child when he was Saul, the Roman. Yet, God used Him in a mighty way. Amazing.

I, like T. Ellis-Ross on the television show *Blackish* believes that forgiveness is about healing what is inside of you and nobody can do that but you.

Un-forgiveness creeps up sometimes. But, I believe you will never change what you refuse to confront and forgiveness is one of those; very similar to an addiction. We all know addictions make you miserable. When I waver, I get too deep in thinking on hurtful things, especially those I blame myself for: addictions, my sons' death and illness, having to leave my young children for doctoral training miles away from home. So, I have learned to just start thanking God for the present day. I thank Him for all the bountiful blessings He has given and continues to give. I begin to thank God for his goodness and mercies.

Most of us have these moments of guilt. We all are human. But, I am reminded of God's grace and sing like Miranda Curtis has instructed us:

> Whatever it takes; I am all in
> I am pressing on; I'll do whatever it takes
> You have my mind, my will...........

Like, Miranda, that is enough for me. Wholeheartedly, this is how I can forgive the person who literally shot my son's head off thus shattering our hearts to pieces forever. The chapter of Mark tells us in Chapter 2 that Jesus performed a miracle or gave us a sign that the Son of Man has authority to forgive all sins.

Most importantly, I never wanted my children, nieces and nephews to grow up witnessing my bitterness with my outwardly un-forgiveness. The world would cause my babies enough pain as it was. As stated in an earlier narrative, I always sheltered or tried to shelter them from my hurt as much as I could. However, as a mother, I will never, ever forget. Life will not let me. And, I know without a shadow of doubt, the shooter and God knows the truth.

I will always remember the last story my grandma told me as a child. She told me how the world would be in my lifetime. She never lied: unforgiveness, fear, hatred, people turning away from God, not being able to know the difference in weather seasons, fathers killing sons, sons killing fathers, greater knowledge spread throughout the world, wars, increase in incurable diseases. These things exist more than ever today; living in fear, especially of each other. More than I have seen in my lifetime, our world today is a vortex of real uncertainties of what the world would become progressively under our present day political clout. Most importantly, we are fearing for our children and grandchildren.

My life experiences have taught me to just run my Christian race so I can deal with whatever comes my way. Everything else follows. I have doubted in my life but always find myself running back to my faith. I have not always trusted in God the way I do now. For I find, nobody can give you peace like God can. I try to lay in that peace. My pastor reminds us that everybody *has sinned and will sin*. We all fall short of God's glorious standard (NLT, 2019). That is why the Lord left the Holy Ghost and church for us so we as His children would be able to endure this life (Rev. McKinley, 2012).

When I think about the last time I saw Tron on my mother's porch, I smile knowing he is with God, my mom, dad, brother and niece in heaven as the bible and my pastors have taught.

When I think about J being cured of cancer, I thank God continuously because He saved my child. He did not have to do it; but He did.

God uses Suffering and Repentance and mistakes. They never drive God away. There is no sin greater than God's forgiveness. So for a peace of mind, I truly forgive the man who killed my son.

The only thing I regret and if I could do it over again, I would have spent more time listening to my young boys instead of lecturing.

In conclusion, I believe, if you try to fill your heart with love for all people, joy, patience, peace and forgiveness, it will result in your actions and work. Other people will say of such a person that she or he is beautiful on the inside. Such beauty becomes visible on their faces and in their actions. Have you ever noticed the faces of people that come "out" of church after church service is over? To me, most of their faces look content or smiling. I always say they are filled with what they need to live in this world another day, another week. They remind me that God is faithful.

The opposite is also true, I believe, if your heart is filled with unforgiveness, covetousness, jealousy, unhappiness, greed, hatred, anger, the bible and research say you become progressively bitter and it truly shows in your actions. Is that you? Do you know someone like that? As Christians, we are told to strive to be a person whose heart is reflective in their actions. As believers, we are told we are a peculiar people. We do not have to covet others' positions or titles. It only gets you deeper in a negative space that is hard to pull out. What the Lord has for you; is for you. *Work hard, prepare and stay focused for what you desire in life. Work for it.*

My mother used to say, "Be happy with what you have. There is enough in the world for everybody."

She would so often remind us of a bible verse: "What is it to gain the whole world and lose your soul?" (Mark 8:36). Put another way: "Does a person gain anything if he wins the whole world but loses his life? Of course not! There is nothing he can give to regain life (Good News Bible-Mark 8:35-37).

—∞—

Food For Thought

You cannot be bitter and thankful at the same time.

Forgiven and No condemnation.

PART TWO –
"IF ALL OF THIS IS NOT
FOR THE GOOD; THEN,
WHAT IS THE POINT?"

Just Another Day That The Lord Has Made Church and Sundays

CHURCH HAS ALWAYS been the cornerstone for Black people and always will be. For the most part, we attend church and are taught to *reverence* the *Word*. I have worshipped at our church for over 50 years (since the second year of its inception). My church is a Historical Black church that history reveals was once a Spanish entertainment hall. It was organized by the church founder, Reverend E.B. Joyner and charter members on the last Thursday in 1966. Reverend Joyner was a preacher, teacher, civil rights and community activist. The *first* church service was held at the Junior Byrd Restaurant and Lounge on 19th and Broadway the first Sunday in 1967. The first Baptismal ceremonies were held at the Galilee Baptist Church, a neighboring church dwelling, until the church pool was constructed.

For me, church was always a place where we learned about life in so many ways. We were taught to love all people. We were never taught division. It is still that spirit filled dwelling place where we can gather to not only hear God's words; but also to encourage and help each other (members and non-members alike). I have so many church memories both good and bad. More good than bad.

We are blessed to have had strong mentors of proud trustees, deacons, mothers and ushers, nurses, youth directors, assistant pastors, musicians and choir ministries serving at our church. Only a few remain today. Most have died or left the church, which is typical for the present day Black rural area community church.

My first life-long mentoring experience outside of my family, relatives and friends was within these church walls. As a young woman, I remember attending the Adult Sunday School classes with a group of senior women in the church. These strong Black women were always dressed to kill or in their Sunday best most times with matching hats. I learned then and now valuable lessons from these wise women. Today, however, one thing I have noticed is that our majority female adult members do not wear hats proudly like our ancestors did. So, I ask, is it because we have forgotten how to be proud in this chaotic, busy and less respectful world of ours?

Man, these church seniors could tell some whispered mischievous or what we call "fass" funny stories when they were not discussing the Sunday School lesson. But, they loved the Lord and we respected them. If children misbehaved in the church, all the mothers or deacons for that matter, had to do was look at them and they would stop and change their behavior right away.

It was already hurtful enough moving through the reality that I had made a mistake early in life. But, my most painful childhood church memory was when an older female member stopped me in the hallway from marching in church with our youth choir group. I remember it so well. I was about to march in the church with the youth singing group and she stopped me and told me that I had a baby now and directed me to sing with the adult choir. As a result of this hurt, I left my church but found my way back later in life thanks to my middle sister who told me to come back to our church. She told me that incident was just an attack from the Devil. As always, my Sista was right. So, I returned to my church.

I am so glad I did because I was able to raise my young boys in church. Now, as adults, they talk and laugh about their own church memories. Isaac talks about how he played Jesus in the annual Christmas plays. Our pastor saw Hakim's musical gift and encouraged him to play the drums in church which only further encouraged his love for music. What I am most grateful for is the biblical teaching and spiritual values taught to our children in church. In my opinion, making sure your children have a Godly foundation is the most important gift you can give them, especially in today's world.

As I look back, my mother's encouragement and the church encouraged me to attend college. My introduction to a Black Ph.D. was in the church. It was when our church founder's son would occasionally visit the church and the pastor would introduce him as Dr. Franklin, and the church audience at that time would loudly applaud. I had never seen or heard of such a person. As a child, I wondered if there were others-especially Black women with the same degree.

After church, there was always something special about those Sunday afternoons on my mother's porch: the laughter, the gathering, the love and peace of just being together. There is nothing I can compare it to. After church, the family, (children and grandchildren) would gather at my mom's house for dinner, family fun and good conversation. Neighbors knew we would be on the porch. Some would pass by the house on Becker Street and blow their horns and we would wave. Some would stop by for the Sunday visit of love and gathering. We would talk, debate and argue over issues like only Black families and friends could. On that porch, engulfed or not engulfed in the conversation, one could just rest, be comfortable and be loved.

Be assured you could always get a full course meal at my mom's house. That was how my mom was raised in the South and how she trained her girls to be. When my mother got really ill and could no longer cook, my middle sister, who is a special education teacher, inherited this task. She continues my mother's tradition of southern cooking family get togethers; especially on Sundays. Sunday meals sometimes includes hot water corn bread, fried cornbread, neck bones, soups and gumbos, greens with smoked ham hocks/smoked meat, pinto beans and rice, fried chicken, mashed potatoes, candied yams, meat loaf, barbeque her b** off, ham, peach cobbler, homemade ice cream and homemade sweet tea, sliced cucumbers, tomatoes (sprinkled with black pepper and salt), sliced green and white onions, pickled beets, and Chow-Chow.

I know what the readers must be thinking – so many calories! But being with family is worth it; listening to their stories, disagreeing sometimes, crying sometimes; just loving on each other; those calories are worth it.

When my mom got so sick and would hardly say anything, we would sit on the porch while momma sat in her wheelchair gazing out the window. We would try to get her to eat. But in her last days, she would talk incoherently or stare out the window, except for the times we would hear her call out to Jesus, her mother, and others.

For many years, I remember my mom and dad sitting together on the front porch relaxing and laughing; mostly on Sundays. When my dad went to heaven, momma moved her seating spot from where she and my dad used to sit to the other side of the porch where her rocking chair sits today. What a time we would have on that porch just going over life issues -whether it was children, work, good and bad times. My mom would most times quietly listen to us with a remark or recommendation every now and then. However; my dad, did not have a problem telling us how he felt on any issue. I miss my dad.

I remember on Sundays and during the work week, my dad would come into the house, wash his hands after mowing his beautiful lawn and my mom literally serving him dinner like a king. That was her man. But, my mom treated everybody the same. It did not matter who you were – friend or enemy. It did not matter. My mom loved you and one could feel that love in her presence. I would take work issues home and discuss them with my mom, especially ones that upset me. My momma would say to me, "So, tell me, what did you do or say to cause or prevent any of that?" She often times worked my nerves with that question. I miss all that. We miss momma, Big Ma, Grandma, Auntie, Aunt Jean, Miss Jean, NaNa, Ms. Ware, Mother Ware. I tell everybody: if you have parents, positive mentors, role models or guardians, treasure them. You are in a good space. Some example is better than no example.

Going back to my church narrative, for some reason, momma always thought her diabetes wanted to act up after church services. I could not convince her otherwise. So, me and my mom would pick up a snack after church before eating a southern meal my sister had already prepared for Sunday dinner.

But, momma loved church, her pastors and church members

unconditionally. She attended and gave as long as she could. She would tell us, "Regardless of whatever happens in the church, you have got to take care of the church like you do your homes." Though, I never saw her write her monthly tithe offering check. She always had us to do it for her. Ok, we spoiled her.

We started performing the Holy Communion ceremony just the two of us (my mom and I) when she was too sick to go to church. Sometimes other family members would partake. However, one of the most precious church memories was when Sister Rebecca would bring communion to the house for the three of us for as long as my mom could sit up to receive it. Another occasion was when the Mission Ministry sent her a beautiful homemade blanket that she would always wrap up in during chemotherapy treatments. She treasured that gift. It is now spread on my living room sofa.

Another memory was when the Nurses Guild church family of two (mother and daughter) would mail the Sunday bulletins to her at home. She cherished the many cards and flowers sent by her church members and friends. She would so often have the cards set apart from the other mail so that we could read them to her, many times while she lay in bed.

My mom loved serving in the church as a nurse and on the Mothers Board. On the first Sundays, the Mothers Board Ministry of wise women sit proudly in their white dresses and hats in the front of the church on the middle pews behind the deacons. Oh, what a beautiful sight.

My mom's church *girlfriend* would stop by sometimes on Sundays after church and mom would always be expecting her on her good days. They would sit on the front porch or in the living room on inclement days and talk like girlfriends. Mom would have us bring her guest a towel to put across her lap and would have us fix her a plate of dinner. And, if we did not fix it to my mom's satisfaction, she would have one of us to return to the kitchen and fix it right. That is just the way she was. The Lord would mostly be their conversation along with every other girl talk you could imagine. This would so often tickle me. I learned a lot.

Momma was a nice lady but she could "go there" with the best of them. If you wanted to talk about relationships, she would. If you wanted to talk about sex, she would. She could even discuss with you the greenhouse effect or what is referred to as climate change today, application of Birnbaum's theory of leadership and views of the different critical race theories because we would rehearse our speeches or presentations for elementary, high school and college over the years with our parents, especially momma. My father became fascinated with the greenhouse effect. He was truly an outdoorsman. So, I tried to keep him informed. I always thought that was so precious. My dad would be so proud of the young people protesting all over the world about the "climate change" issue today.

My mom went through many a degree program with her children and grandchildren, especially the doctoral, superintendent license and MBA degrees. Many times we would have our laptops with documents spread all over the front porch discussing what to add or take out of documents we were preparing for school. We would even debate theories, like whether to reject or accept the null statistical formulas, empirical versus other statistical concepts, multivariate regressions (causal effects), predictive analysis, etc.

Momma would be right there in her rocking chair looking over us or adding her comments. Most of those study times, would be on

Sunday when guests were gone and our children playing outside or all over the house with my mom yelling at them, "Ok, break something, if you want!" The kids knew she was a "softee."

I remember in her last days I had to write a grant to keep my job and would work on it sitting next to her bed at home or in the hospital. Every now and then she would add her voice to something that I was reading to her. That voice began to grow dim and the bedroom and hospital rooms became quieter and quieter. We all knew what was ahead of us. The hardest thing we ever had to do was take care of her during her last illness and bury her at the end of life. What I do know about death is that suffering cannot compare to heaven's gift. One time, unexpectedly, we heard momma in a comatose state, shout out "Master!" to the top of her voice. She stretched her hands upward as if she was reaching. Then she slowly rested back on her pillow.

It hurt. But, I truly realized, momma was close to receiving her heavenly mansion prepared just for her.

But, the last church memory of momma was when our pastor, Reverend Reginald L. Johnson, Sr., visited her at home. He grabbed her hand and began to pray for her. Well, she pulled her hand away. Pastor was so hurt. He looked at me wondering what he had done wrong. Later, one Sunday after church, I told Rev. that behavior was just a habit she had in the last days of her heavenly transition. She did it to all of us. I told him, literally, what she was saying to him and us was, "All is Well." Pastor smiled. She loved her pastor. He loved her. She called him, that "*Little Boy.*" Like no other, that little boy eulogized my mother. He sang her favorite song while we ushered her remains out of church to the Sandusky Street burial grounds singing, "He Is An On Time God":

He's an on time God, Yes, He is (oh oh oh)
On time God, Yes, He is
Job said
He may not come when you want Him
But He'll
Be there right on time
I'll tell you
He's an on time God, Yes, He is

(Dottie Peoples)

In my opinion, pastor's most intriguing sermons included stories about biblical women. There are many wonderful stories of biblical women. However, my favorite ones are of Rehab, Deborah, Ruth, Mary Magdalene, Esther; and, especially the Virgin Mary story. I have always felt like Mary (the mother of Jesus) knew my most pivotal pain, "*a mother's pain.*" I just know she knows all of our pains.

Christian television is fine for some. No one can shout or cry louder than me listening to televangelists like Pastor Parson, Pastor G.E. Patterson or Father Pacwa, Fr. Pisegna etc.

However, for me, there is nothing like the gathering of the saints in the church. Our church theme: "A church of love, faith and unity."

The church has a corporate anointing (J. Prince, TBN, 2019) and the gates of Hell cannot stand against it.

Food For Thought

Seek the Kingdom of God First.

Righteousness is a gift.

Grace – No Condemnation. Repent.

The _Word_ says to "assemble" (E. Gilmore-Williams).

Our pastor - Rev. R. Golson, Sr. sings....
"I've Got A Mind To Live For Jesus All of My Days;
You Can't Stop Me, You Might As Well Join Me!"

If the Lord is God, follow him. (1 Kings: 18;21)

"You Ask Me Why I Do What I Do?" - A New Black Educational Science Paradigm Approach

I BELIEVE FAITH not tested cannot be trusted. Man, have I been tested! If you want to know what pain feels like, ask me. Wholeheartedly, I believe my pain has channeled my personal and work passions in life. Some may disagree. For you see, it is the only way I can rationalize why I do what I do in the sometimes irrational ways that I do it. What I find so unique about my career in education is the fact that my work experience, education, training, researching and writing centered on a place where I was most familiar: Gary, Indiana. My home. My community; a place I knew. This type of community work demands an irrational methodological approach.

My personal desire has always been to help with the cultural, academic and social conditions of people; particularly people of color. Truly, it has been my calling and my protest. I hope others will join.

More than ever; I believe without a doubt, a structural science(STEM) teaching approach is the only way people of color (especially poor children) can begin to escape our present and predicted educational, employment, and societal state of affairs.

Further, I have been told in different ways to cease waving the k-12 and undergraduate science/STEM movement flag because my community efforts appear to be somewhat *fruitless* in Northwest Indiana.

Forwarding on, I just believe our culture's economic, social, educational and financial negative strongholds will change with science instruction. Most of us (especially our children and grandchildren) will not be able to compete for today's high paying jobs without major *strategic community science help*. Think about it.

I understand this effort or paradigm shift will require a ***major-holistic-cultural hands-on, educational intervention.***

I have faith in my race.

Science unpreparedness will always have generational widespread impacts. Covid-19 has pushed US science, technology, engineering and mathematical secondary and post-secondary educational lack out for the world to witness; especially among communities of color. For example, according to Dr. Oz (2020), only 5% of US doctors are Black men and more Blacks die treated by White doctors than Black doctors! We all are cognizant of the cultural, economic, social, educational historical disparities among the races. All we have to do is look around us. But again, this disease has pushed this academic lack out front for all to see. Research reflects that US 12th graders test 40% below the academic base in science and 46% of K-12 test below average in STEM skills (NAEP, 2015). ***Therefore, Therefore, some how,*** *some way, we have got to arouse the consciousness of the Black and Brown races to what academians, science experts and politicians are telling us with their writings and oratoricals regarding the nation's STEM/science education/training unpreparedness; especially among communities of color k-12 secondary schools.*

A lack of diversity in STEM will lead to fewer discoveries, which means fewer, and potentially less viable solutions to humanity's most pressing problems (GERI, 2019). Empirical research findings continue to recommend and direct us on the urgency of our children and communities learning STEM/science subjects. It tells us specifically that they will further be left behind without this knowledge.

As a community, we should be shouting about the lack of this education and training from every local, state and government roof top!!

This is my life-long calling. Readers, by now, you know *"I Love The Lord"* as I have in first person shared some of my life stories in this book.

The Separation of Church and State Laws limited the inclusion of my own personal religious views and opinions while researching and writing my academic and job assignments. We all know how that works. However, I was able to use what biblical writers reference when they cite the Jewish veil being torn into when Jesus died on the cross [Matthew 27:51] by comparing this construct to the then newly educational movement to educate freed Black slaves after the 1863 Emancipation Proclamation Act in my dissertation work [DeNeal, 2008]. Slaves needed to be re-trained. Most did not have skills beyond the dominant culture's farms and cotton fields. So, W.E.B. DuBois and Booker T. Washington took bold and unprecedented actions for those times to re-educate the newly freed American slaves.

Both trailblazers risked their lives. As history depicts; the dominate US parties, did not want this non-prosperous move to occur.

Accordingly, I argue, we are at that point in society where we have to teach science to our race or be placed back on those same mental and even physical slave fields soon.

A federal survey found that high schools that had a majority African-American or Latino enrollment were less likely to offer math and science classes at all levels except algebra 1 (Office of Civil Rights, 2018). This is a major cultural problem for us. Further, I and others will continue to argue that our race; especially our youth is "**not**" prepared for present and future US and global science, digital and technology jobs that would prepare them for life-long careers.

Based on where I live, work and research, many do not see hope because of long periods where they are unemployed and having to work in part-time jobs (mostly essential jobs e.g. food and retail) all their young and adult lives to daily survive. This has become the norm. Enough is enough!

I just believe my assignment for now is pushing STEM education in the Black community; praying that other cultures will become involved and we all work together to make this work. We might as well. We all are in it together!

Most importantly, we all know there is a major American Technology Revolution occurring today. Therefore, in order for the Black race to compete for jobs; we must be science or STEM trained for today's digital market and economy.

Research shows that the entire nation's science knowledge is very limited as compared to world-wide data reports. As a culture, we need to be teaching science (STEM) across the boards. This would be a major educational paradigm shift; unlike anything we have ever seen. A science/STEM education and trade would add value to the Black and Brown US populace in so many ways. I am reminded of Dr. Martin Luther King's words, "*And we are coming to engage in dramatic nonviolent action, to call to the gulf between promise and fulfillment; to make the invisible visible* (1968)."

Therefore, science education is the critical value and should be "given" to our youth. No parent should allow their child to live without it. There is too much software out there (Khan Academy, Project Lead the Way, New Jersey Simulated Robotic Surgery, etc.) for this not to happen. As a matter of fact, in addition to secondary schooling, our children can be science/math homeschooled after school, weekends and holidays in this manner. Families can learn together. We cannot blame everything on the school system.

IMPORTANT NOTE

Today, STEM related career opportunities are among the fastest growing of all occupational sectors. America will fall short of demand for these highly educated workers by millions as early as this year, 2020. Therefore, we have got to find ways to ratchet up this important call and implement science practices across all African American platforms, especially in secondary schools. You have got to believe we can do this together.

This new way of teaching will require loosely and tightly coupled efforts between local communities e.g. correctional centers, trade and vocational schools, public, private, charter schools, colleges, churches, mosques, Greek organizations, NAACP, Urban League and other

MY MOTHER'S PORCH

civic and social organizations, municipalities, etc. This is going to require a complete change in how we teach, preach and perform in our communities. We are the DuBois(s) and Washington(s) of today. We have to do it ourselves and now is the time – push **science, technology, engineering and mathematics education and training!**

Our re-newed Black STEM/science education and training must be bold. Our initiatives must be energetic and imaginative. We have to teach our children how to control computers. We have to teach them how to be digital literate so they can deal with this society. It encompasses so much e.g. history, critical thinking, etc.

Stacy Abrams, Yale law school graduate and author reminds us that poverty and science-mathematics economic inequality is a danger to society. It is a documented fact that the lack of science knowledge is a problem deeply rooted in our culture. It is indeed problematic for our children when our country remains at the bottom academic percentiles as compared to other nations. A small group of us believe we can overcome our uneducated science populace, particularly for low-income and first generation children, with early and often educational science and math preparedness.

Our kids are smart and have the talent to lift themselves up out of poverty with strategic, mentored monitored science progressive training. But, it is harmful to be smart and gifted with no opportunity, with no look-a-like mentors and no real world science and major math hands on experiences. Mentoring is one of the most important tools we have to empower and uplift our young people to ensure they have a bright future. Research shows Gary is a targeted poor demographic area. As, we all know now, poverty in America is almost impossible to escape without help. We can begin by coming together and designing educational STEM/science model schools that infuse science instruction

62

across the entire school curriculums, thus preparing students to "think science." We must engage and monitor our children's progression at all times and not let this become a "failed" educational process.

We know, science and innovation is all about discovery and has the power to break negative generational strongholds, especially financially. The country did it when they needed a science trained populace during World War II while at the same time attempting to remedy the wrong done to the American Asian population. Data reports indicate that today the Asian population is overrepresented in the US STEM fields (Pew, 2018) while people of color continue to be underrepresented in the same workforce. Research shows educational opportunities were provided at that time while underfunding science educational efforts for non-traditional populations. This was war time for the country and the government needed scientists. So, history shows that roads were cleared for some to become science educated. Not everybody.

After World War II, the country's push for science education declined and that is why the country has fallen so far behind other counties academically, especially in science. Also, literature proves one cannot be literate in science without the same wisdom in math.

Who can argue that science training is urgent based on the fact that we are becoming aggressively a digital society and only a few people of color occupy these jobs? My son shared with me that he has only worked with one woman in his profession as an IT Software Technician!

Today, as we become more technology automated, fewer part-time skilled and unskilled jobs are becoming available. When part-time jobs become so competitive, then what?

Yes, the stock market is historically higher than we have ever seen it. Of course, it is driven by digital assets mostly. Who is involved in this digital economy? Not us.

In this regard, STEM training for the Black masses is so important regardless of how one tries to rationalize its economic benefits. Most of the wealth during the past two decades came from these investments which further widen the gaps financially between the rich and poor. Ironically, the Internet was started with government funds. Yet, only a few people of color have benefited and profited from digital/computer industries. "Think Black" scholarly work was written by an author who grew up in the IBM world clearly depicting some negative powers in this industry. The author lays out how the Black race would benefit from technology training.

Economic reports display economic disparity gaps are getting wider. We can begin to close this gap with science (STEM) education and investing which allows citizenry that contributes to the common good. Something has got to be done with inequality rising and student loan debt at an all-time high.

Most importantly, it hurt when I realized how my parents struggled in poverty and academically. I really wanted to be an engineer and did not know how to pursue this dream. I always wanted to work with my hands, building stuff. I wanted to solve problems. **But God, had other plans for me in a whole different direction.** I ended up in the field of education. Education is a unique field. It allows the bold to dream. My Purdue University Instructional Design Degree showed me how to embrace my passion for building and designing educational curriculums.

However, as a child, I loved reading Greek mythology.

My favorite Greek classic story is the *Clash of the Titans*. I even included excerpts regarding *Medusa;* who is an outcast God in the story of *Clash of the Titans* in my dissertation work [p. 41]. I used a qualitative approach grounded in theory to illustrate and highlight the *similiarities* and *differences* for a sample of Ph.D. Black women at varying institutions:

> Surely, of all creatures that have life and will, we
> Women are the most wretched.
> Still more, a foreign women,
> coming among new laws,
> New customs, needs the skill of magic, to find out what
> Her home could not teach her…
> But the same arguments do not apply to you and me.

I have no regrets pursuing an education degree. But, I do wonder where an engineering science degree with an emphasis in Greek Studies would have taken me. I have a niece who is an engineer and she wears the title well.

Nevertheless, the best opportunity we can give our children is to STEM train them before they graduate or leave high school because today our world is one that needs either science (STEM) or technology validation skills throughout. As stated, it has been predicted that future jobs will continue to be limited without it. But, we cannot force this learning on our youth or can we?

I will never forget my mother's cardiologist who was born in the Middle East. My mom loved him. He was such a patient man. He loved my passion for a STEM school in my hometown. Upon one of our doctor visits, I asked him about his motive to be a doctor. He jokingly; but at the same time seriously shared with me and my mom that as a child he and others were told that they *would* become doctors and were strategically <u>matched, mentored and trained</u> by medical professionals while growing up in their own communities. His childhood story further encouraged my science calling. But, this science calling and effort is truly hard work in my community with so many other educational, social and economic issues taking precedence.

Most importantly, we all know, we cannot force our children to learn or do anything. We are competing as parents and educators with so many other issues for their attention e.g., social media, etc. However, if children are enrolled in science/technology curriculums and/or initiatives early in their secondary education schooling; they also will have that same chance as my mom's cardiologist of becoming doctors or successful in any other STEM field of their choice.

Chances are good, if we are able to enroll them in a professional controlled environment, provide teachers that look like them, infuse science/math in all curriculums, hands on work practices, monitor student progression and remediation from k to 12th grade and summer before first year of college. They will have a significantly higher chance of succeeding in today's STEM world of work. I do know, the earlier and more often you do something, the better you become of it. This training should start in kindergarten.

Really, all our children need to read and write about positive STEM role models like scientist Katherine Johnson who was a Black American mathematician whose calculations of orbital mechanics as a NASA employee were critical to the success of the first US space lift. This story is told in the 2016 biographical drama film *"Hidden Figures"* movie portrayed by some talented Black female artists. Also, children need to read and create science projects about inventors like Heidi Lamarr. History reveals that Ms. Lamarr was an actress in the 1960s. However, she became known for inventing the Navy's schematic force that filtered today's Internet. History tells she did not receive a dime for her invention. We need to teach our children to research and write about soldiers like the first female African American soldier surgeon Lt. Gen. Nadja West (Ret.) former US Army Surgeon General and our very own, Gary bred and raised pediatrician who is heading our city's pandemic crisis while caring for both of his parents with the disease.

Our children need to read about Dr. Kizzmekia S. Corbett, a Black viral immunologist who is one of the lead scientists in developing a vaccine for today's pandemic: Covid 19. Research shows her work on defeating this virus started long before this specific disease surfaced.

Her and other medical professionals of color work and visibility is so important. Science education and training among our culture is so, so needed when Blacks are three times more likely to get a Covid virus and three times more likely to die from it. Presently, over 46% of our population is unsure whether or not to be injected with the newly approved (2020) vaccine because of our country's historical medical past practices and racism *(e.g., Tuskegee Study of Untreated Syphilis in the Negro Male, etc.)*. Moreover, research is limited regarding the impact this new vaccine will have among the children.

Also, children need to *read* about and *remember* the science works of Dr. Anthony Fauci who has led the HIV medical protocols and fields for 30+ years. He continues to lead the US in our current fight against the Covid-19 disease, even under political negative pressure. He has no problem announcing to the world the works of Dr. Corbett and others who look like us.

Children, read, read, read - "People going to use what you do not know against you (C. Harris, T.I. - REVOLT, 2020)."

Science history builds bridges and shows us all how to improve as a people and how to take care of each other.

Finally, somehow, we have got to clear this science learning path for our own Black communities. Everybody's science approach will be different in their own communities.

This is a lot of work. One person in the community can make a difference. But, I believe a well designed church and community grassroot science effort would be the most effective approach for this urgent science education call for a time such as this.

Most importantly, funding science efforts are critical where you live or the targeted community you wish to support. ***If we show increasing positive results, other funding will come.***

—∞—

Food For Thought

"I feel good knowing things are in such good hands." (Andrew Young-co-author of Civil Rights Movement) – [Sister Circle Show, 2020]

Establish cultural value for our race.

Survival: What I learned From the Streets of Gary To The White Ivory Towers of Education

I COULD HAVE stayed on welfare for the rest of my life and ceased attending college. But, an incident with a welfare caseworker and my father's dislike for "*handouts*" (he called it) or public assistance made me further determined to finish high school and college to help provide for my family. My father worked hard to keep his seven children and wife out of the public welfare system and we never were. He believed a person should work (if possible) for a living and all who did not work and slouched around did not care whether they ate or not. Some would say that this notion is old fashioned and outdated. But, it was always logic to me. Why wouldn't one want their own?

Anyway, at one point in my early undergraduate college life, I was eligible to receive food stamps, a medical card and a welfare check. As a matter of fact, my caseworker told me if I did not stop going to college and get a full-time job, she would take my welfare check from me. I refused and she transferred my check to my mother's name. So, I worked hard to get off that government system.

Many years later after finishing school, I saw this caseworker in one of the local stores and I introduced myself. I reprimanded her for telling young women not to attend college. I told her the worst thing a caseworker could do is not support those individuals who wanted a college degree to better their family economic conditions. I explained to her that it was hard enough being on the welfare system while taking care of children and studying for a college degree. I explained how hard college can be without having support systems in place; particularly through the first year of college for women with young children.

Also, I could have settled in *no good* relationships. I could have become a drug addict or prostitute. Our hood environment certainly had these opportunities available. Oh, *But God.* Thank you for *grace!* He did not have that planned for me. "The streets ain't made for everybody. That is why they made sidewalks." (Taraji Henson)

I received my first college certificate and two-year degree when I was 9 months pregnant with my last son. I did not want to participate in my first college ceremony. But, my mother convinced me to rent the college robe. I could not zip it all the way up over my big stomach. But, I made it work. I noticed there were not many people of color in the graduation march and only a few in the audience. I felt like I represented so many working, struggling women of color that day. My three- year old niece was concerned about my pregnant condition. She broke away from her mom, ran up to me and asked, "TeTe are you ok?" The feeling I had looking down at her face overcame me. I knew I had to continue with my education, no matter how hard the struggle. My niece and so many others would pay attention to my educational walk.

I would go on to receive my undergraduate and graduate degrees. My baby sister and I graduated with doctoral degrees together. My younger sister started the program after me with her *smart self.* Our college graduation was held on the grounds of the college campus on a warm and bright sunny day with hundreds of attendees.

The ceremony started with all of its grand ceremonial formalities. But, surprisingly right before the doctoral degrees were announced, *NaNa* handed me her graduation number ticket in order for me (her *Big Sista*) to walk across the graduation stage first. It caught me and the announcer off guard.

But, with tears in her eyes, my committee chair slowly announced both Ph.D. graduates. My mother was so proud. Never boastful, just proud.

I have only worked at two college institutions over my 30 plus years in higher education: at a community college and a 4 year graduate institution. Therefore, I trust that I can speak to my educational experiences with some degree of credibility. I just pray that my voice makes a difference.

First, let me say this. I worked with some outstanding co-workers during these years in higher education. I met life-long friends. Moreover, I was blessed to have met and worked side by side with so many talented people to meet 2 and 4 year post- secondary educational objectives over my tenure.

As mentioned, I remain a community activist for science k-12 instruction.

<u>Critically</u>, some of us believe the major science educational k-12 challenge for the community is students not passing the 2-year college test assessment tools; specifically, the fraction sections. This is especially true of students from my community. Before retiring, my colleagues pressured the college to remedy this problem that caused this college admission denial; but, to no avail. During my time at the institution, rarely did you find Black or Brown faculty of color curriculum members from the city of Gary or surrounding areas. In my opinion, missing were the curriculum contributors/designers who were highly likely aware or experienced in community influences (both negative and positive) that impacted most of the students being taught at the college. With that being said, most faculty and leadership live outside of Gary. They would come to work in the city and go back home.

Many of us worked with students and witnessed how several lacked foundational math skills that prevented them from enrolling not only in our 2-year community college but; eliminated any and all possibilities of completing a math and/or science program degree at any other post-secondary institution.

Conversely, many Gary high school graduates do apply with high hopes and dreams but become frustrated after being turned away by mostly negative math assessment test results. Nobody knows what happens to these students. Many after their college admission denial do not see the benefit of trying to enroll in college again. It broke our hearts to see students walk down the institution's hall away from the Testing Center looking at or balling up their paper test results. This is a deeply rooted academic problem for the city and potential college students. It will continue to have generational wide-spread negative impacts in Northwest Indiana until the city, secondary schools and colleges work together to address this long standing educational problem. Gary seems to forget that our students most times are attending school and "surviving" at the same time. Citizens, this is something to protest about!

No one can argue that probably most of these students do not know how to manage the college process and have not associated with mentors of the same hue (e.g. teachers, doctors, lawyers, scientists, male teachers, physicists, ones that could direct them socially and academically). In many cases, students do not have professional relationships (mentors) inside or outside the home that would help build their self confidence, teach the value of work and teach how to compete for high paying jobs. Data reflects that our nation has unemployment rates ranging from 6.7% to 13.9% among the American races (Bureau of Labor Statistics, 2019). Who are they talking about? Gary's unemployment rate is over 70% in some areas before the pandemic!

Today, in my neighborhood, over 80% of Gary children are low-income and first generation, poor children. Today, many of these households are headed by single women. Many of our children are being raised by grandparents and foster parents. The negative impact of the community's foster care system needs a closer review and changes. Gary's children see and live in crime zones as in other similar socio-economic groups at alarmingly increasing rates.

Literature refers to our community college as an "open door" public college system in our state, an educational system for all residents.

In my opinion, the institution has moved so far away from this ideology. As stated earlier and *according to this institution's Institutional Research Center empirical data, students predominately fail this institution's college entry assessment due to poor math scores; particularly high school math fractions and are not allowed college admittance. In my opinion; this in fact, is not an open door college system as counterparts continue to claim.*

Additionally, standardized testing contributed greatly to our public school academic demise. Data shows that children test scores are disproportionately lower in schools with high rates of poverty; communities in economic hardship. In recent years, the standardized performance-based assessment concept was introduced nationally. The school corporation was warned by the Educational Talent Search TRIO Program professionals in the late 90s [DOE approved mandated objectives]. But, to no avail.

Standardized testing is so unfair in so many ways. How can you use a normal bell curve to show mastery without taking into account actual knowledge? The Gary school system was not prepared to embrace this new process. As a result, any gain in student academic progression would be eliminated by poor test scores. It remains true today. It is hard for our nation to let go of this unfair racially biased practice.

We have a high - high school drop-out rate and the lowest English, math and science test scores in the state, an unstable charter school system with none performing at a consecutive 70% pass rate for any five-year Indiana budget cycle. Nevertheless, it appears that these schools are allowed to compete over the number of students that enroll in their school for the monetary gain – not student's academic gain. We have a public school system that has been taken over by the state, no school-wide online educational training capacity at all, a high youth homicide crime rate, no safe parks, no movie theaters or no skate board parks. Unfortunately, Gary, indeed is depicted as a bad place to live and bring up children. The news media speaks to the nation's drug overdose problem today. I want to remind everybody: our community has always had that problem! Our children live all this. They live and see so much failure around them and social media does not help.

In my day growing up in Gary, our teacher/mentors helped us the most not only academically, but socially as well. We had teachers who cared about us and more importantly, looked like us. Once, we had a community of strong Black and a "few" Hispanic teachers. Back then, we had strong teacher/mentors like Mr. Bhampion, Mr. Myles, Ms. Piske, Ms. Green, female Coach(s) Codd and McDuffy, Mr. Aldridge, Mr. Staples, Ms. Ford, Ms. McKulough; so many others that we will not forget. These were teachers who lived mostly in the community and ones that we saw and respected five days of the week. We knew them. They knew us. More importantly, they knew how to teach and behave us. We dared not run home and tell our parents about a spanking we received at school. We knew the high significant chances of it happening again at home, but worse. As a child, you knew it was going to be bad when your parents were called to the school unknown to you and you walked in the classroom and there your mother and/or father sat at a desk next to yours!

My Froebel elementary principal spanked me one time. But, first he gave me the choice of either him swatting me once or sending me home to my mother for my "smart mouth" issue as he put it. I do not have to tell you my preferred person of choice to spank me. It was not my mother and that was for sure.

Many teachers pass through Gary with no idea of how to teach children of color; no idea of their growth and development, no idea of any Black Student Development Theories (Nigrescence Model or the Black Racial Identity Model) that helps to identify the educational stages a student progresses over time in education. A good teacher is always likely to be a good researcher which is what our children need along with science training.

Some may even have prejudged our children as criminals, especially Black boys.

Our goal should be that every high school student be STEM trained at graduation and/or 100% college placed.

I say to those boastful secondary and post-secondary schools, "Do not just publish your successful accomplishments with no empirical data to back it up. Prove it."

Gary's tax base does not support continuous updated educational resources as predominate well off schools. As stated, most times there are no large school swimming pools, updated version of computers, latest textbooks, science camps, supported athletics, art, music programs, debate teams, etc. These schools cannot give the students the current well-rounded education they truly need for lack of resources.

Finally, to area educational institutions please do not take me wrong for my views of our educational systems and practices because I love and preach the life-long benefits of receiving college degrees. I am building my own personal testament with my continued community field work. I know my subject area and I am attempting something different to contribute to education.

White Towers

Higher education has been my training. In my view, institutions (both k-12 and colleges) and local industries in our area are loosely coupled entities (existing independently). I believe all parties would benefit if outreach efforts were made with the mission of preparing targeted community students in 9-12th grades for local jobs e.g., medical, engineering, researchers, technology, male math teachers, etc.

This would give our children a chance to receive the training needed to compete for high paying jobs at home. In addition, I believe companies that hire students as interns, externs, volunteers should help eliminate some, if not all of student college loan debt for degrees earned while working for the company; e.g. MBA, Medical, Laboratory, Engineering, Ph.Ds in Health/Science.

Additionally, push for students of color to move into STEM degrees upon entry into your higher education institutions. Why is it that all three local post-secondary institutions are only graduating low percentages of student of color with medical, nursing or other STEM degree. As stated, yet you boast of your enrollment, persistence and graduation rates?

I know everybody does not feel the same way I do about a science education and training. Nevertheless, we have to give students educational opportunities to compete in this competitive digital job market. It is not a matter of if we can do it. The questions become: how do we do it? What science models do we use as a race in our communities? Through this pandemic crisis, I have watched how the predictive science models work to warn, measure and produce outcomes to fight this disease. I cannot help but to think about how simple elementary predictive analysis instruction could be taught to our children while they are mostly at home under the present unprecedented Covid-19 circumstances. This one lesson, I believe, would encourage them to think science; especially as they watch the daily news announce these predictions.

But before any science proposal, we can begin by making sure Gary children are trained in fractions. In my day, the community college's Student Services Department professionals and leadership would have resolved this problem immediately. It would not be a major community issue today.

My belief is that we should be teaching our kindergarteners online classes, coding, beginning algorithms and robotics! Reinstate Science Fairs and start Robotic clubs and compete because our lack of incentives or fear of science and math has affected us generationally.

Not to know is bad, not to wish to know is even worse – African Proverb.

Theoretically, I believe science education should start early because the progressive learning process demand periods of time. It is up to us to inspire this learning and not just by lecturing either. Science training is power and we must create and provide this power for our community.

Also, all our children need lessons in financial literacy and second languages e.g. Spanish, Hebrew, etc. I believe, for the most part, we did not receive these lessons and therefore most of our children certainly do not have the wherewithal much less the understanding of learning the overall benefits of finance lessons. How I wish someone had taught me about investing, contributing to retirement savings starting at a young age. As mentioned, the stock market today is at an all-time historical high with technology leading the way. No one told me had I invested $20 per month before I became 20 years old that I would be a millionaire at retirement.

Reports show that our gross national product is not stable. Of course not, many college graduates are swamped with student loan debt, stuck working in part-time jobs with short life spans and in unstable full-time job positions. Therefore, most cannot make purchases that contribute to the economy (purchase of homes). Most rent or live with their parents. Sadly, Black Americans continue to remain at the lowest rate of home ownership (40%) compared to other American races (US Bureau of Statistics, 2019).

You do know the government is stable enough to wash away student debt every 7 years like in Israel biblical times and not feel the effects of it? We help everybody else globally. The US spends trillions on defense. This amount would eliminate most of US poverty. In my opinion, this would be true reparations! It would help us build bridges rather than walls.

Also, secondary educators, take the children out of their Gary surroundings. Travel. Participate in Science Olympiads. Establish STEM clubs, robotic clubs and add monetary elements for attendance and grade progression and see how this will change things. Take them to Chicago plays, operas, professional basketball games, college tours as grade incentives. Teach them to do community work in the city. Protect them. Do not allow them to be bullied stripping them of self-esteem and educational opportunities.

How can students be advanced and prepared for education or the job market when most do not have computers and printers at home? Gary has a sharp digital divide!

Gary citizens demand that secondary, post-secondary and the city government leaderships correct barriers that prevent our student's educational progression; like the policy that "denies" high school graduates admission to the community college because they cannot complete fraction problems. To be fair, simple fractions should be mastered by the student before entering the 9th grade. This should not be an academic problem for any student in their first year of college. If you know this is a major educational stumbling block problem in the community, fix it. In all fairness, this long term problem needs to be eradicated. Students who were denied enrollment over the years for this reason; especially first generation local area students, should be re-contacted, mathematically tutored, and mentored for community college admission. They should not be instructed to an on-line math session without teacher instructional assistance.

As stated, math teachers and other staff members witnessed and rebelled against this negative admission standard. Some even got in trouble for voicing and writing to college leaders regarding our math admission testing concerns.

We realized that this added educational barrier was one of several for mostly community low income, poor and first generation students seeking a college education.

I complement our community college system for inventing and supporting the Dual Credit Program. It was an East Chicago campus CAD-DRAFTING professor Dr. Sharles who invented and started the Dual Credit college bound relationship many years ago. Back then, this old college process was referred to as "Tech Prep" at the East Chicago campus. Today, many high schools and colleges practice this community college's innovative concept. So, let's debunk the notion that this renowned secondary/post-secondary educational process was started and implemented by a Gary charter school. It was not.

Students now can graduate from high school with a high school diploma and college certificate. Students who continue on to college will have 30 or more transferable college credits under their belt. This process is the best secondary/post-secondary process since the Gary high school vocational training days started in the early 70s. Dual Credit should benefit so many more students. So, should the 21st Century Scholars Program as well. This program provides a full four year college scholarship for Indiana low-income children.

The Northwest Indiana colleges support TRIO government funded programs that have academically, socially, and economically supported Gary's first generation, low income college bound children and adults over the region. The community college has maintained their institution's programs at the Gary and East Chicago campuses for almost 20 years with proven successes. Thank you!

Additionally, we need to implement history, religion and multiculturalism classes across the board (high school and college), allowing us to learn all we can about each other. It is not fair when two little sisters from India cannot attend a local surburban Predominately White middle public school without being harassed or bullied. Multicultural Fairs should start as early as kindergarten. It was not until I taught college level Multiculturalism/Religion/Racism that I really learned how other races contributed to our US society. For example, the Japanese in the US has an American slavery history and were placed into internment camps. I learned that Japan also had a Christian Underground Railroad to hide Christians during a time when thousands were martyred for their Christian faith. Research shows that the Mexican-American race is known for its collectivism among all other races in America.

Data reflects there were over 60 million Native Americans residing in this country in 1492. It also tells us that this was America's *"First People."* Today, that number has decreased to 6.79 million in 2018 (US Census Bureau). Yet, they still hold on to their Indian identity.

Finally, four- year higher education institutions: please mentor, educate, train and promote your own professionals of color. You recruited and hired them. You know them. Do not be afraid. Communicate with them. Listen to them. Trust them. Things you see lacking, address. Remember everybody cannot be a servant leader as suggested by author Robert Birnbaum. Put these professional men and women of color in the classrooms at your institutions. Put TRIO, Student Life, Diversity and Student Development trained professionals in administrative leadership positions. That is how you begin to mirror diversity in the workplace.

Presently, many institutions continue to grapple with the subject of Diversity and attempt to resolve or display cultural sensitivity by implementing Multicultural Centers with management teams of color in leadership roles, annual Diversity or Sensitivity Workshops and a month or less cultural celebrations. In my experience, it is going to take more than these efforts because we have a continuous systematic institutionalized racial problem in our society that needs to be addressed and not covered up again and again.

The unfortunate fact is that many do not or pretend not to see racism as a problem. Research depicts that racism exists even among cultures of color (Banks, 1989). Our US climate certainly points to this fact.

Millions of dollars are being spent by institutions on different diversity trainings. The university would benefit more by compensation and promotion. For example, when I left the community college, a young Black part-time gifted Chicago medical student taught Anatomy and Physiology and Aquaponics' (gardening without soil). I have seen students line up to be tutored by this professional. Further, a young White male worked in Gary for the first time, witnessed the needs and wrote the first minority male grant that increased persistence, retention and graduation rates for this population over the college rates for three consecutive years. Interestingly, the college eliminated both practices under new leadership.

Neither were recognized and promoted by the college. It was no concern to the college that their instructional talents and tutoring efforts helped the institution increase the Nursing School's pass rates over the years. They both are no longer with the industry. Students lost.

Conversely, some research reflects that Multicultural and Sensitivity Workshops only further divide and weaken institutions. *I totally disagree.*

The fields that should be the most diversified are not. Our country needs ***Affirmative Action*** programs more than ever to help level the different fields for all citizens. The absence of women of color in college leadership should give the industry pause. Some realize that these women have the hardest time being promoted to chancellor positions beyond the community college level. It is unfortunate that my experience and color played a determining factor in my promotions, especially among male leadership. I never understood it; but, always realized my stance as a Black and female when it occurred. But, I never understood it. I always believed and was trained to believe that even in the case of differing viewpoints (that being the case) there should never be outright long-lasting division(s) among college coalitions (AAUP, 2007) to the degree that it *hinders* progression of overall missions of the university. The impact of it causes deep wounds. One should not be intimidated or harassed at any time.

College leaders need to support their own professionals of color to help the university diversify and help move generations of students through their academic pipeline academically, socially and economically, regardless of the college atmosphere, which can only be done with institutional support. These well trained professionals of color have walked in different shoes and are one of the university's greatest assets. They are the faculty of disciples who will ensure the continuity of learning.

The world of education can be traumatizing for some at times, and this is one of the reasons that educational institutions should be operated by a good leader. What is a good leader? A good leader is one who listens. He/she is also one that knows IX laws like equity and fairness. He/she is able to demonstrate their vision through their walk, talk and performance, not through fear and authoritarianism. He/she is one who is able to get the buy in of others to accomplish agreed upon mission(s) of the institution. Nothing less.

They lead by example. *I am convinced, a true leader must be a servant.*

Real heroes resist power. They fairly distribute it. For me, as an experienced Black educator, college and university leaders (in many cases) often overlook the educational founder's real mission for higher education and that is to successfully serve *all* students; not just a *selected* few.

Fear, envy and jealousy, which all overlap institutional racism are running rampant in higher education like they do everywhere else in our society. It breaks my heart to say that. But, it is true. Negative coalitions can be a strong force if allowed to fester. Negative coalitions are most times negative, unhappy people. True leaders can pick up on this negativity even when these coalitions perform their cowardly acts through other people.

A good friend and TRIO colleague, a passionate educator in the prime of her life committed suicide in her office on a Northwest Indiana college campus on a Sunday morning. This shattered our lives.

She had shared earlier and often that no one seemed to care about the institutionalized racism and frequent racial attacks she suffered from a college personnel while serving low-income k-12 students. What a loss.

Finally, I thank God for my mentors. I do not know how I could have survived higher education without them (Y-Jean Chambers, PUC past Ombudsman -deceased), Gary's Urban League past president Eloise Gentry (deceased), Chancellors Bole, Chancellor Haltierra, and Chancellor Soley. Thank you! Our community college system in Gary is better because of your work when you served at the helm.

As we all know, this world is becoming progressively darker and our world would benefit from the contributions of professionals of color, especially at the doctoral level. Ph.D. training is a necessary condition. It is necessary for the survival of the American university and credibility of work for the accomplisher. There are many of us seeking or willing to seek education out here, educating ourselves and empowering others so that the future of our children is better than most of us are living today.

In pursuant to the recent college admission scandals in our country; we all know that is nothing new. Somebody just got caught. Understandably, we do what we can for our children. But, when it comes to education; especially for the poor, disabled, Black and Brown students; we have had government funded educational programs like previously mentioned TRIO programs for decades to help us through secondary and post-secondary educational pipelines. Thank God! We just have to work and keep them as part of our country's educational fabric.

Thank God for Historically Black Colleges and Universities (HBCUs), faculty, staff, students, parents, mentors and benefactors. (Lift Every Voice and Sing-J.W. Johnson, 1871- 1938) These are accomplished institutions that not only the Black race; but the nation is proud.

—⦻—

Food For Thought

"Teach One to Reach One." (Queen-Cosmetologist, 2019)

How to be a better mother or father, how to handle conflicts or bullying, dangers of alcohol and drugs should be taught first and continually at home. If so, these students are likely to do well in school and life.

Challenges, Challenges – Use The Hurt

God tests us before He trusts us with success.

EVERYBODY FAILS SOMETIMES. I was dropped from my Ph.D. program. I could not pass the doctoral statistics examination. I passed the manual hard parts of the tests like building ANOVAS, multiple regressions, etc. But, I could not pass the computerized section. Test taking is not easy for everyone. I tried three times. I was devastated when I received the letter from the school that I had been dropped from the program. While I sat out of the program, other students and instructional staff were complaining about this particular examination. So, the college decided to eliminate it from the doctoral curriculum.

Meanwhile, nobody knew the stress I was experiencing at home during that time. I was working full time in supervisory capacities. I had to help take care of a sick paralyzed brother. I was raising boys without their fathers, etc. My mother knew. I had spent many hours studying on her porch while she watched my children. I never put my worn statistics book and class notes away. I tried to write an appeal letter to get back into the program. I never finished it. Everything pointed to the fact that I was done. I prayed, got quiet and waited patiently for something to change.

Well, one day a professor, another angel in my life, wrote me and explained that the college had approved a conditional re-admission for students in my situation. I wondered: how many looked like me?

That condition was to pass Descriptive Statistics with a grade of B+ or better. I was reinstated back into this educational zone. I was so humbled by this second chance. I not only passed this class; but, found myself tutoring a few of my classmates. I was the only Black in my cohort. Can you imagine? I was fully accepted back in the doctoral program in Cohort II. I started in Cohort I and ended in Cohort II.

In my day, the doctoral program was fairly a new program and learning statistics and final writing examinations were performed manually. I believe both should be done in the same like manner. Sometimes, technology is not the best method for teaching and learning.

I tease aspiring doctoral students that Cohorts I, II maybe III were the sacrificial sampling groups for this institution's newly formed Ph.D. program.

Technology played its part in advancing the program. No longer is it required that doctoral students manually learn statistics. Instead, calculation results are now done by statistical software programs. Also, interestingly, doctoral students preliminary written exams are now administered as take home tests.

We, the earlier cohorts, had to sit in a private room alone for a period of time and manually handwrite the test answers for three consecutive days. We were not given a computer, dictionary or any other source to use for this examination.

I remember one semester a professor gave us a case study to critique and summarize individually. He placed us in assigned groups. I received the highest grade and the other students decided not to study with me. I was told by the group leader that I had made the highest score and they came to the group consensus that I no longer needed their help.

I struggled, sometimes too embarrassed or stubborn to ask for help. We, the earlier cohorts were taught by Sister Sarah; a nun. She would encourage us with her smiles, upbeat character, strong critiques and kind remarks on our returned papers and other classroom assignments. Sister knew how hard the first sample cohorts struggled; especially me.

When I finished the degree, I emailed her and she responded, "I knew you would." A third of the way through my program, I was introduced and matched with a full-time tenured Black female professor, advisor and activist. She knew her stuff. Dr. Z. suggested to me my mental and educational weaknesses, recommended remedies and gave me her timeline for me to get this program completed. It was on and she did not play with me. Dr. Z. was so proud when I received my degree. Only Dr. Z. knew my personal and job related problems. This mentor characterized for me how a Black female educator should endure in the good, bad and ugly times of life while pursuing a professional degree. She believed in my work and what I wanted to achieve in my own community.

At that point in my life, I was *determined* to complete the degree. One other male student of color was in the first cohort. But, he later dropped out. The institution recognized my persistence and determination to complete this process. A nearby private catholic school allowed some of us to stay in their vacant nun's residence hall to help reduce costs for overnight campus visits. I have no idea who arranged this special accommodation. I will be forever grateful.

Dr. Z. was the first doctoral professor of color who taught us in the program. So, we welcomed this new faculty member's instruction, insights and perspectives. She taught us the importance of examining higher educational issues and complexities through our own lens........ *"from the viewpoint of the college balcony (so to speak)."* We knew Dr. Z. was limited in what she could do for us as a newly hired faculty member. We understood. This professor, historian, author became a mentor for so many of us; one or two happened to be Black. However, my institution has yet to give her the promotion she truly deserves. As stated, before her, I found myself very lonely at the school. I earned my degree while experiencing "the other" phenomenon (Hamilton, 2009). I felt alone until this new mentor that not only looked like me but had the expertise I needed to be similarly trained. The intersected and intertwined barriers of both **race** and **gender** plays its role in our society. But, the *otherness* which I grew to understand and acknowledge; became an inner strength at every level of my career and education. It is not that I felt completely powerless at any time. Lord forbid. To the contrary, my *otherness* Black identity helped build character. It was more so a confirming inner strength to endure. I know that developed survival characteristic *"strength/trait"* came from growing up in my community. I did not realize while growing up as a career-minded little Black girl, sitting at my little wood desk on the "Border" side of Gary, that I was actually preparing or being prepared for my life long work. As a young girl, I often wondered if I would complete a college degree. But, did not see it for me. Nobody close to me had a college degree. This is a lesson to be experienced, written about and taught. These are stories that must be shared.

Today, a graduation ceremony portrait of me, Dr. Z. and my sister is on my fireplace mantle. *"For there is nothing that God cannot do."* Luke 1:37-NLV

Now, let me be very clear. I am proud to have graduated from a nationally known doctoral program where I was included in the first college sampling cohorts. Further, I am proud of the doctoral students of color my institution continues to groom.

I am not berating my institution *at all*. In so many ways did the institution support us. For example, my advisor allowed me to come home to help bury my oldest brother during a summer on campus required assignment.

Once the funeral was over, I stopped by my mom's house before heading back downstate to school to take my oral final exams verifying expected knowledge of the Ph.D. academy graduate training. After talking with my mom on her front porch, I kissed her and started out the door. She immediately called me back, prayed and blessed me from the contents of her familiar bottle of blessed oil. I returned to school.

The very next day, the president of the college and a doctoral fellow administered our individual oral final examinations. That morning, I prayed while walking to the tall Education Building where the test would be held on that day.

My prayer was that God and the ancestors would acknowledge the *"tedious"* long doctoral road me and my family had traveled; and to grant me this mountain top blessing by directing my thoughts and guiding my oral answers.

I remember being so nervous before the test started. But, later my nervousness relaxed and I found a comfort zone in answering questions by highly esteemed scholars. The first question was asked by the president regarding the institution's hesitation to move forward on different college issues and I paraphrase here. I took a deep breath and begin to answer from a personal perspective and backed it up with my favorite research that I had become familiar over the years. In response to his first question, I answered, "because of a fear to be professionally different, the failure to listen to all constituencies and most importantly; a failure to change........."

I defended my work that day.

The president stood up and stated, "That is it. The test is over," after the first test question asked of me. The other professor in the room calmed him down and we continued with the rest of the examination.

When the test was completed, both asked me to leave the room for what I thought was forever.

Finally, the door opened and they invited me back into the large room and asked me to be seated. They both congratulated me, "Dr. Angela Smith."

Oh Happy Day.

Thanks to Chancellor Dr. Sole (chancellor of the community college), who believed in my work and who recommended me for the program.

Today, my work and credentials allow me to stand on my belief and what the founders of education believed the purpose of higher education should always be: **to teach, to learn and to serve.**

—⟨∞⟩—

Food For Thought

What is for you; is for you!

**When you become successful at anything
in your life; Remain Humble.**

*God's love and assignment does not impose burdens upon
us that we cannot fulfill. For whatever He asks of us,
He provides the help that is needed (John Paul II).*

God answers by time; not theory.

PART THREE –
WHAT DOES LOVE
GOT TO DO WITH IT?

Our "Black Love"
Has Been Wounded

AS A YOUNG girl, I longed to see people of my hue on our first black and white television set. I remember thinking, where are they? What I did not understand then was that the mass media was not interested in positive stories of our cultural life unless it involved negative connotations. It was not profitable. This was media producers of film who were and still are predominately White. Most times we saw Blacks and Latinos in roles such as Hattie McDaniel, as *Mammy* in her character in the movie *Gone With the Wind* for which she was criticized by her own race.

I questioned this too as an inquisitive child. My parents tried to explain Black entertainer survival and I tried to understand how we as a people had to survive. However, I never ever felt one had to succumb to such roles that were being depicted on television by Black folks. It concerned me that television did not show roles of some of my hue that I saw sometimes in my community like Black men and women teachers, librarians, Black married couples, police officers and fire fighters.

But, for the most part, we were happy to see colored folk in roles on television and in books because it was rare that we did. One always raised an eyebrow of attention when it occurred. Nobody knew and certainly it was not included in my history lessons at school or home that Hattie McDaniel was a charter member of Sigma Sigma (Sorority) Chapter and was awarded the Motion Picture Academy Award for the best supporting performance of the year. Soror McDaniel was the first Negro to receive the coveted Oscar (White, 1974). She served her community and her race. Not only Soror McDaniel, but other entertainers of color at that time survive in the entertainment business but; not, at the risk of their own race being defamed or put to shame, even at a time when the Black face was painted and laughed at. The *"Blackface" form of theatrical makeup used by non-Black performers* surfaced in our country after the Civil War. These characters demeaned and dehumanized Blacks in media performances. Today, as a result, such performances would have lasting negative ramifications. Cicely Tyson's long professional entertainment career should remind us all that we do not have to accept any role that *"belittles"* our culture. In her words, *"Just Keep It Going".*

In today's world when I see predominant negative roles being played out in the entertainment business industry; especially with the music and video juandras - it shows old fashioned me (some would say) that our youth need lessons in positive thinking. Negative music has so drastically changed our culture. We have gone from a culture of entertaining roles whose intent was not to defame to one that does just the opposite. I am old school and not the expert in hip-hop or rap music for that matter. All I know is what I see and hear. And, I do know I am not either a Hoe or Bitch! I worked hard not to be.

This portrayal tells and reminds me that we as a race have not come that far over the decades when in 2020 our youth of color portrayal of a servant mindset of materialism, possession and greed overpower their common sense. How can our youth and young adults consistently offend each other; especially in public view?

Our youth need to be reminded of the stories of their ancestors being stuffed in ships from their homes across the seas, chained and forced into inhuman conditions for profit around the world.

Our ancestors sacrificed for us. However, today, many of our youth take these "uplift" sacrifices for granted. In that regard, many of our youth are growing up in a world having a materialistic mindset and slowly growing out of love for each other, which is illustrated in today's music. Competition is good until you take the love out of it. The Motown Industry is an example of love.

Today, the current negative music has reached a level of degradation that is beyond understanding. Unfortunately, it goes back to the beginning of this narrative where I say medias or corporations are collecting profits while we have bought into the mentality to dance and sing to the beats of our own destruction.

A mindset paradigm shift is needed among the youth. I believe, our children need history/multicultural lessons to remind and teach not only of our struggles but the accomplishments and struggles of all American races. Data reflects that our nation is becoming darker and we need to learn about each other (values) like never before. We must teach about the immigration and enslavement of our own and other cultures because many are still in cages! Children need to be taught about the Mexican Revolution (1910-20) and Trail of Tears (1831).

We can begin to defeat the defeatism spirit of our populace which has always overshadowed us. Whether in willing or unwilling ways;

we have played into the spirits of selfishness, greed of others and among ourselves. This mentality in itself continues to allow ones to be caged and have limited freedoms.

Let us not forget, our Black ancestors tried to hold it together. Love and support of each other helped with that over decades. However, competitiveness and jealousy among the culture is running rampant. Unfortunately, it has led to the aggressive slandering of each other for self-benefit or self-gain. *In the same vein, if you bully and say hurtful things or take anything that is not yours, you will never be happy or content with it. Think about what you had to do to get it.*

Our past Black performers never defamed our culture or each other like our youth are doing today. We, as a race, which includes the church need to understand why loving each other is so hard for us.

Lovelessness is a societal problem and it has always caused so much division among us. In my opinion, it is all about power, profit, greed with rising populace views and falsehoods that travel faster *and* believed more than the truth. Can't our young people tell? Lessons on the Black struggle can be taken from many sources. Again, I believe these lessons, especially on Black fatherhood and survival can be taken from Black comedians like D.L. Hughley, Bernie Mac and others who worked to move the races through their comedy on the subject of the Black struggle. Any struggle, as gospel entertainer BUZZLE says," Is better with God."

Here is my personal plea. First, please tone down the degrading music. Second, today there are a few more rich and famous men and women of color than ever before who can share their wealth with the less fortunate. Therefore, there is no way our nation's children of color should be suffering academically, socially and economically like they are today. There is no way our children should not be in science training preparing for STEM jobs. It would be amazing if they are taught the algorithm necessary to build their phones or perform a simulated robotic surgery starting at an early age instead of video games. Can you imagine how this one learning approach would excite our children for a lifetime?

It is critical that we all do our part, if we have not already to make sure our race of children become scientifically trained for jobs before they graduate from high school and help the poor in our neighborhoods with our own individual talents and resources. Say what you want about Kanye West. He got the message. He and Chance The Rapper are performing in what they refer to as *Sunday Services*. They are making the message clear to all who want it - *Believe and Serve*. Whatever gift God has given you, give it back to Him.

Life should be easy, automatic and one should take challenges for whatever career opportunity they want to pursue. But do not hurt people. I am sure our most well- known artists of color took many chances to become successful. However, the truth of the matter is life is not easy for most of us. We, so often, find ourselves in this world "fending" alone. Everybody has to struggle.

But, just remember, "You are called to your purpose." (R. Adeleke, 2021)

Congratulations entertainer Common for establishing your school in Chicago. Congratulations to Angela Ye on The Breakfast Club. I say, "You are a lady. Overlook the haters. Keep informing us. Do not change."

I agree with the entertainer Jay-Z when asked about a controversial football player's questionable behavior. He replied and I paraphrase,

"Let us move on to the attainable" by letting all people know and the world know, we cannot live by our individual collected goods alone. Congratulations Rihanna on your outreach work!! My mom loved Jay-Z.

Congrats to Beyonce' for becoming the first Black woman to have 100% investment in her own clothing line. Thanks to all who are working on the criminal justice system to release our populations of color from institutionalized cages (prisons; especially in Indiana – especially in Northwest Indiana). **Forgive and help them.** Poverty is expanding. Remember, the rich are getting richer and the poor are getting poorer (Houston Chronicle, 2019). Today, over 70% of US women and children are living in poverty (Dr. Rev. William Barber, 2021).

Even Apostle Peter got a second chance after the crucifixion and you know what he did. Jesus even healed the ear of one of his haters on His way to the cross for him.

Most importantly, Peter was granted the honor and opportunity to share the Good News to the first church. But, if you read the Book of Acts, he still had to be reminded from God to do the right thing on three different assigned tasks. I am no saint. As I shared in an earlier story, I too am working on *me*.

Let me go back to my earlier narrative before I went off on this tangent. Again, we have become a society of greed. The US does not suffer from scarcity. It suffers from greed (Rep. Jayapal, 2020). People cherish material success as the sole measure of value and meaning to life. Most of our young people never had it. Most do what they have to do to take care of themselves and their families. Survival makes a person do things sometimes when they know in their hearts it is wrong to do, believing that when the respected systems fails; then it is ok to make up your own.

The *streets* can be tempting and luring. Pray.

I say, our young people need good stable jobs they can depend on.

They should not be made to settle in different low level jobs either. Presidential candidate Yang states the most commom job in America is a retail clerk (R. Maddow Show, 2019). How sad. People, we have got to turn this trajectory around.

Again, today, recent economic job predictions demand training in infrastructure and IT jobs. In many cases, you do not need college degrees for these type of jobs. If people in the community do not have high school diplomas, do not turn them away. Help them get one. Send and pay for them to attend the Career Centers to learn these trades. Some educators have a problem incentivizing education. I don't; especially for the poor. I believe, education, training coupled with goodwill should be rewarded. Provide stipends for their attendance and grades (see TRIO Upward Bound model). If you truly want to uplift our young men especially today, give them educational and training opportunities coupled with monetary stipend experiences and see what happens!

Mass incarceration is a larger issue than we talk about when more men of color are in prison than in educational training or college. There are just too many men and women of color in correctional centers; especially youth. We pray that newly proposed reform laws will change this situation. Infrastructure and IT Technician training should certainly be in these institutions so the imprisoned can have some type of hope for a career opportunity upon their release from these institutions.

We can prevent our young people from sinking into a deeper and darker place, bullying, killing of each other, overpowering and defaming each other.

The one lesson in this narrative, among many, is to understand that in the absence of a stable emotional God fearing foundation, material attainment or privilege easily erupts. Obtaining access to material privilege or stuff never satisfies the needs of the spirit. Only love can and it will show in your work.

One Black writer writes...."Those hungers for materialism persist and hunt us and we end up saying, taking and doing things to each other we should not." The bible describes this as "covetedness." We seek to satisfy our endless consumption for materialism and power with appetites that easily turn into addictions that can never ever be satisfied. Needs of the physical body can only be put to rest when we love and care for our souls.

Our ancestors knew love and togetherness was the key to their survival and thus initiatives like the Underground Railroad, Sojourner Truth, abolitionists emerged. All the abolitionists were not Black either. History lessons vaguely show that other nationalities and their families hid runaway slaves underneath and inside their homes, teepees, churches, barns and helped finance Underground initiatives as well.

As mentioned, after the Civil War and Emancipation, Booker T. Washington and W.E. DuBois picked up their educational mantles and debated over what schooling was best for the newly freed slaves. Most could not read or write. Legislations and prohibitions of South Carolina had passed the first laws prohibiting slave education in 1740.

Washington believed industrial training should be the foundation for Negroes to add value to society. DuBois believed the function of the Negro should be a college education. Those brilliant academians knew that masses of slaves had to be trained and educated to survive because they no longer were tied to the slavery of the cotton fields. So, through Washington and DuBois's tirelessly work which included authorship, advanced liberal arts education and emergent trade schools were formed to educate free slaves.

That was that time.

It is our turn now. America is in a different place and different time. Young people you are the "Now Generation" and with that title comes responsibilities. I believe you are the catalyst for "science" change.

It is urgent that we teach a science based and/or science, technology, engineering and math education and training. Listen, a quantitative and qualitative reasoning science education emphasizing computation and data analysis taught to our children is the way to go. Our brilliant cell phone and video gamed populace "educational light switch" will be turned on. We will see this unfolding right before our eyes.

All the students will not study comprehensive and significant modes of inquiry of the same STEM subject. But, all can and will learn the ways of thinking or method of analysis associated with a science education in order to live more effectively in an environment that will forever produce more science and technologies. This in fact, will prepare a young person for a life-long career.

Therefore, I encourage everyone, especially our talented artists (mainly because you have the platforms that have so much influence over the youth) to join this major science movement. Help us get our Black, Brown and Indigenous communities STEM/science educated and trained.

It will take our whole village to start this science movement.

So while the world is embracing the daily political catastrophes of impeachment, elections, world civil wars, climate change and today's global pandemic; as these major issues are being unfolded, we should be focused on urgently science training Black children. They matter. Remember, the poor cannot help the poor.

It is urgent that we work for the rising generations. My recommendation is implementing an inclusive STEM secondary school in every rural city for our children's sake even if you have to start in a storefront or basement or church basement!

That is showing real *agape* love or putting love into *action*.

Only a movement or conversation that is provoked by desires can eliminate the educational inefficiencies that will continue to generationally impact us all.

Your gift may not be implementations of science schools or science initiatives. Whatever you think it takes to help move our children socially and academically, let's do it and do it now as a community.

For now, the whole community (parents, young adults, children, pastors, teachers, organizations, etc.) need to hear and understand the importance of this science call.

If, we as a community, stand up, voice our concerns, opinions and demands, things will have to change soon. When young people rally, adults listen. Again, it will take the whole village to start and continue this movement. Please do not get me wrong, social justice and protest is required. Do stand up for what you believe in. I believe, you do not choose to get into a movement; you just do. But, I repeat, a return to love, action and service is crucial for our culture and society as a whole. With action, we can do something about the reported social, educational and economic conditions for a large percentage of our people which leads to so much stress and anxiety, heartache and human deterioration.

So, this is not a stand for any movement away from today's equity/political movements. Instead, this is a Black and Brown science education call and plea to be added to the demands. But, unless love is the force that undergirds us as a race or culture, deterioration of our God-given ancestral bond will continue to shift in negatives ways. Sadly, today we see it happening all over the nation and world. But, when everything else works against us, love will keep us. Without love, we have nothing (D. Pearson, 2019). When you love, it flows. I say do not worry about the naysayers. Just do not let your enemies have the last word. How? Stay positive and continue to serve. Your enemies will not be able to handle that disposition. Expect it. It is okay to be a "hugger."

In my opinion, we just need to double down on loving each other; especially now. Again, while everybody is watching today's catastrophes unfold before our eyes, our communities of color should come together to make sure our children are prepared academically for digital and science jobs as we move forward now and certainly after this pandemic. Of course, you cannot do this until you find out <u>why they are so angry; especially with themselves and treat the problem.</u>

Young people, you are a chosen generation. The prophets wish they could have lived in a time such as this (Luke 10:24). You do not need a validation for *Whose* you are! You were predetermined and predestined to do your work. Therefore, we cannot do this work divided as a race. Young leaders; especially in the church, "Stand Up" for science STEM training in your communities.

Nobody knows your neighborhood like you do. None of the incarcerated, no child for that matter should walk away from correctional centers and high schools without a STEM/science trade, certificate or college degree.

If we do not do something, data will continue to show educational deterioration or educational lack in our areas of low income and first generation populations, especially in science and math in a time when they need it the most.

Remember, love begins with "self- love." How in the world can you love someone else, if you do not love yourself? Try to forgive, you will feel better. Let Grace do its job. Another thing, laugh more. The bible says laughter is good for healing. It further states, laughter and love give us wholeness and health.

Many people have issues with the bible and its parabolic content. But, I run to that book that sales more than any other every year. I run to the first book that was ever printed. I run to the Word. When I feel myself growing bitter, critical, negative (it happens to most of us), I read my favorite bible scriptures and say my favorite prayers - Psalm 1 and Psalm 23, Our Father and Hail Mary.

In conclusion, choose love. Choose healthy models of self- actualization with the understanding that when we love ourselves not in an arrogant way, we are positioned to love others. Put another way, when we have self-love it shows in our lives and we are able to love others. Some may think this human characteristic is a sign of human weakness to be exploited. I beg to differ. When we have strong self-love, anything that demands self-martyrdom or limits our spiritual growth is recognized and dealt with early on. The bible calls this discernment.

I am human. Christianity is a daily walk. I heard a preacher say one time, "God has a big calendar. But, there is only one day on it - *Today*."

Sometimes you could hear my mom say when she awakened in the morning, "Lord, thank you for today."

—⋈—

Food For Thought

You have more influence than you can ever imagine (Dr. D. Grier, IMPACT, 2019).

Love? Look at Congressman Elijah E. Cummings's life story. He had a profound impact on all of us to the end of his life! He courageously fought for us. He served and left us with this quote:

"Through your pain, you will find your passion, you will find your purpose."

Whatever talents you have; use it - Worship Always. Remember the Lord's Day. Keep it holy.

Read, research, learn what makes people of color beautiful.

LeBron James, Michael Jordan, Tyler Perry, Don Lemon, Joy Reid, Lester Holt, Robin Roberts, Michael Stragan, Gayle King, Rev. Al Sharpton and so many others; thank you! You all are professional role models for our Black and Brown young people to mold their lives after today.

No matter where we live, we are in this together.

My Hometown – City of Hope

I GREW UP in Gary.

The city of Gary, Indiana was founded in 1906 by the United States Steel Corporation. Gary was once a prosperous steel city populated with a diverse culture of citizens. Recently, the city of Gary was voted as one the most miserable cities to live in by a media source. I say that belief is in the eye of the beholder. Some do not know this city like the ones that were born and raised here. No, I would not walk down the main street in my city or any other city for that matter at night. But, Gary is home for many across the country and world. In my travels, I always smile when someone else talks about those good old Gary times when they find out my hometown. Many people share similar stories of what it was like growing up in this community once.

Gary, Indiana

Let me tell you about my community, the city from where I hail. Gary is not the most miserable city. It was and still is made up of generational faithful citizens, their children, grandchildren and other citizens. In earlier times, many migrated to the city. In the early 40s-early 70s, Gary was a prosperous place for innovators and entrepreneurs to start their own businesses, find work in the local steel mills and educate their children.

Regardless of stories told about Gary, it was and still is a place of hope and beauty in many of our eyes. It is home. It is a city with rich resources, beautiful trees, a beautiful lake front with wonderful sand dunes and wonderful people. There is nothing like driving around Marquette Park Beach where lakefront houses sit on a warm sunny day; especially on Sundays gazing at the blue lake water and distant shores of the city of Chicago.

Gary is adjacent to the Indiana Dunes National Park and borders Lake Michigan. I have spent *"many a Sundays"* (as our elders would say) riding around the Miller beach front listening to my favorite radio personalities like *Sundance on Station V103, the famous Jim Raggs and Herb Kent (deceased)*. This is what me and my mom did when she was with us and what I still do today.

But, the most important jewel of the city of Gary is the fact that there are outstanding committed citizens that help keep the city together because of their love for their hometown. As a child, we lived in a diverse community where there was a Greek bakery around the corner, a Hispanic Store on the corner, a Black Lounge two blocks over and a White car sales shop across the street.

We had and still have fraternity and sorority organizations that do extraordinary community work in the city. The ***Gary Sigma Gamma Rho Chapter***, for example, has been committed to the community for 95 years, approaching their 100 year road mark with the mission of service, as in all the other Greek organizations. In 1924, *Sigma Gamma Rho Sorority, Inc.* chartered the first Negro Greek organization in the city of Gary (D. Hood-Harris, Basileus of Graduate Chapter, 2020).

There are other established groups of civic and social organizations (Negro League of Women, Eastern Star, Urban League, NAACP, Book Clubs, Performing Arts, Miller Beach organizations, Sin City Motor Cycle Club, Brother's Keeper, Serenity House, Sojourner Shelter, etc.) in the city. The city used to sponsor an annual Summer Jazz Festival on our beach front. People would come near and far for these well-known safe festive family activities. You could feel the pride of the citizens; the people, on those city joyous occasions. Memories.

I have witnessed, like so many others, the city's outwardly physical beauty demise over time. I remember when the downtown area that now sits in deterioration was so beautiful and full of life. I remember the downtown stores which I thought huge in my child eyes like the Goldblatts Department Store. When we visited this store, I would proceed cross the store alley to enter the Food & Furniture Building where the delicious pastries were displayed, my favorite. Goldblatts had the best salted peanuts and chocolate graham cracker cookies ever. I remember the Farmer's Market where my parents would take us as children to purchase fresh fruits, vegetables and together select our Christmas trees over the years.

When we bought our house on Becker Street, my dad planted his own vegetable garden.

I also remember the Hurich and Haller Furniture Store, S.S. Kresge Department Store, Comays Jewelry, Coney Island Hamburgers (the best hamburgers ever), Gordons Clothing Store, Nipsco, Water

Company, City Hall, Gary National Bank, First National Bank and the Memorial Auditorium Stadium where most of all the high school basketball games and tournaments were played which also now stands in ruin. As a child, I thought the Froebel School Library and the downtown Gary Public Library were great places to visit. There was always something mystical about libraries to me. I would sit on the floor between the book aisles, read books and look at the pages of large journals that had captivating pictures and big words. I remember the Big Bens Shoe Store and the Sears Department Store where my parents could purchase three children dresses for $10.00 and two pair of shoes for $6.00 for school, church and holiday functions.

There were beautiful buildings and houses in Gary as far as we could see or be allowed to see, especially church and school buildings. Presently, there are over 30 school buildings that once sheltered generational legions of students of all races as they journeyed through our city's known educational pipeline now standing empty.

We learn a lot on beauty and barber shop days. Upon one of my beauty shop days, a retired teacher told us pointed stories about the city of Gary. She remembered when the school buildings were strategically placed to keep races within the Gary city borders during a period of time. She told us that in earlier years, Blacks were not allowed to go into neighborhoods pass the Glen Park section of the city which now consists of several abandoned buildings, storefronts and homes. I found this very interesting and probably would use this information in another book.

While she continued to share so eloquently about the Gary School System's formation over the years and her life as a teacher/counselor, I thought as she spoke how retired Gary school teachers could help our deteriorating public school system with their expertise, knowledge and learned wisdom; all of which the present school leadership appears to lack. Looking around, she had no idea the barbershop/beauty shop young and senior clients listening to her and receiving the power of her words. I often think about how we would take my mom to her local beauty and barbershop where she was known as "NaNa" by the young owner whom my mom completely adored. The clientele loved her life experience stories and her funny jokes. But, as this Gary retired teacher articulated her "beauty shop" beautiful stories, much was learned.

Be careful about the words you use or the words you allow to be used (Maya Angelou).

Also, I remember Dr. Chobe's office where our family would visit during our childhood and some adulthood for medical treatments. While serving as an educator in Gary, I found out that Dr. Chobe was a tough advocate for Gary children in places like our state capital for many years. He represented the city and the school system for as long as his health would allow. He would make house calls when my mother was too sick to go to his office like he did for so many other poor families in the neighborhood. He sent a message to me by my oldest brother after hearing I was no longer in the doctoral program. The message - "You did not want the Ph.D. bad enough." That message broke my heart. I finished school before he passed. I also found out that he had placed the article about me and my sisters that stated, "Three Gary Sisters Graduate with Ph.Ds." in his lobby. I found out later that other small businesses in the community had posted our pictures on their walls like Coney Island on 25th Avenue. Some of my students and friends shared this news with me. We were happy to be part of our community's pride.

I remember the Roosevelt and Palace Theatres. The old Palace Theatre sits in ruins today on the Broadway main street. Artists are beginning to draw beautiful murals on these buildings with some depicting the history and struggles of the city.

Recently the first black mayor for decades was eulogized. Artists recently painted a mural of this mayor on the main street. I remember reading his city-wide original plan (The Arroyo Proposal) as a city urban planner employee. Mayor Hatcher had high hopes for Gary. Our first female mayor inherited our city's woes. She believed in a science school for her community when no other city leader did. Now, a new mayoral leadership has begun. I remember his pre-election speech regarding science and math city initiatives. Presently, this new mayor in his first year of serving in this capacity is dealing with the most threat we all have witnessed in our lifetime - the Covid 19 virus.

This is an unusual coronavirus that by its pure nature has stopped the entire world with its powerful wings of mass destruction and out of control deaths, ushering most of us into the corners of our homes in fear and isolation of each other.

Going back to the story narrative, the old Roosevelt Theatre on 13th and Broadway Street was converted into a Pentecostal church. I would attend church services with my aunt. It no longer exists. My aunt used to take me there when I was a little girl. I remember church women dancing around me and something spiritual overtaking my body. I believed that was my first spiritual experience.

True story. When I was a little girl, my parents took us to see then Senator Robert Kennedy travel through our *Border* neighborhood when he was campaigning to be president. I remember standing on the edge of the Adams Street curb holding my Aunt Ava's hand in crowds of people. Men in suits and ties drove and walked beside a black limousine carrying Senator Kennedy as he campaigned in our city to be the next president. He was waving to the crowd of bystanders. As the limousine slowly passed me and my aunt, the senator looked down at me and reached for my hand. In return, I did not hesitate to grab and shake his hand as we looked into each other's eyes. It felt like a dream!

As children, we knew of the Kennedy family. My grandmother even had President John F. Kennedy's picture (his brother) nailed to her living room wall in Mississippi. But, as a child, never would I have imagined shacking hands in front of the old Adams Lounge in Gary, Indiana with Robert Kennedy.

I remember being in the first class of 8th graders to integrate a White school across town on 5th Avenue. We had to be bused. This little girl from another race called me a "Nigga." Everybody got silent and I got confused and ran home and asked my parents what this word meant. My parents finally explained to me why my father had to leave his home in Mississippi. We really never talked about it. That was always a *grown folk* conversation.

But, finally, I understood why he had to leave and later send for his young family to join him in the far North in the early 50s [p. 3]. He refused to be called the same.

So, Gary, once a city full with a vibrant community of small businesses, a renowned secondary school system/curriculum modeled after the Froebel Plan with a "play/trade school" curriculum, a trade school, two hospitals, libraries, good schools does not exist anymore.

Visitors know when they are in Gary passing through the northern toll gates; by the sight of the US Steel Mill that has stood tall on the middle diameter city loop structure intersecting with the main Broadway Street since the beginning of the industry. History reveals that the steel mill and the the city was built on sand and rocks. Upon entering the city with such a known reputation, one will quickly juxtapose a picture of an old city scene of rural beauty to one of real present-day urban decay. Our city carries a heavy burden.

Now, the city that thrived at the height of the steel mill and family owned businesses is littered with vacant homes on many streets. I remember our city being infiltrated with gangs, drug wars and the White flight that contributed to the demise of this beautiful place.

Fear of living in the city has crept in and for solid reasons, I admit. When fear creeps into anything, it weakens hope. For those of us that did remain after so many relocated elsewhere; see our beautiful community deteriorate right before our eyes in a matter of a few years. Now, we can only share story narratives and pictures with our children and grandchildren about the beautiful city of Gary back in the day. We went from a welcoming town full of diverse citizens' eager to work in a mostly steel mill prosperous city to being the murder capital of the nation. Today, that title is leaning our way again.

True, Gary has gone through some turbulent times. But, we still have a sense of community. Therefore, I cannot end this story narrative without speaking to and thanking the Gary community innovators and entrepreneurs that once owned or still own small businesses that trained so many of us.

In my rememberance e.g. the 25th Avenue Coney Island Restaurants, Village Hot Dogs and Polish Sausages, Winters and Powers Construction Company, Moses Excavating, Willie's Garage, Herman's Garage, long standing funeral homes, houses of worship, MaMa Lucy's

Grocery Store, Ruthies, Blue Room, Adams, Two Talls, Bears lounges, 7th Avenue Tacos, Rays Shrimp houses, Beas and Lovell's and other beauty/hair salons and barbershops, Gary and Tolleston Auto Body Part shops, Beach pharmacy & Cafe, etc. lists a few.

We had youth mentoring and training opportunities available to us not only by these small businesses, but also by our local vocational trade/career center and the CNA Technical Center headed by Mr. Harry Banks (deceased), a community activist and social worker. There was a John Will Anderson Boys Club on 5th Avenue and Madison Street. We even had city governed summer jobs available to us in the 11th and 12th grades of high school. This was my first real professional job that left a life-long impression on me.

I will never forget Mrs. Fuoder (owner). She was a sharp dresser who taught me how to dress for work and manage money. She taught me how to type on a manual calculator while holding a pencil in my right hand for hand balance. Yes, I find myself typing that way today. I am grateful. So far, I have not had trouble with my hands and I continue to do what I enjoy: scribbling, researching, cooking, gardening, bird watching and riding around the beachfront.

Also, many of us attended the local Career Center to learn a trade in high school. Many chose beauty school, automobile, accounting, nursing and secretarial training. I chose secretarial training and attended in the 12th grade. I also still use my short-hand skills today; especially in the margins of my bible at church services.

In addition, we have a strong Christian, Muslim, Jew, etc. community. We are most definitely a community of faith. Even with the migration of citizens and the ruins of beautiful church buildings, religious groups still meet and worship in Gary.

I believe, now is the time for people of color to invest in this city and turn it into another Atlanta, Georgia or up and coming Detroit, Michigan which both suffered the same social, educational, economic plight. Their story is a testimony of success and a committed community.

Some may say we do not have the wherewithal to make this happen. I say, there we go fearing and not teaming up to make this happen. We should make Gary too busy to fear and hate. We have more to gain than lose.

Today, when I drive through the city, it appears at a distance that things are happening and changing infrastructurally. It really does.

All of a sudden, our Lake Shore Dunes Park was named a National Park. It is the 7th most visited national park in the country. City roads are being repaved. New bus stops and street lights are being installed. The old water tower is being demolished. The city looks cleaner.

Gary's resources like Lake Michigan with its beautiful landscapes, sand dunes, flowers, forestry and beautiful trees are profitable city assets. They always will be. I cannot help but to feel, something or someone is re-birthing our great city.

———⟨∞⟩———

Food For Thought

Sundance, the DJ, dream is to perform in Africa (Sundance Show, 2019).

Speak it; see it.

Final History Lesson

WHAT IS TRUTH? For one, it is the ability to be a trusted messenger for the good of any community or people; which in fact is earned by telling the truth, even if it hurts.

Histories of all Americans should be told fully, truthfully and preserved for future generations. Our youth should read more. They should learn from each other and make eye contact.

We have to continue to teach Black History lessons to our children. Remind them that it was the White Lions Ship that docked at Virginia Colony's Point and traded some of their prisoners (Black slaves) for food on August 20, 1619 (Hulton Archive, 1619). Some say 20 slaves were sold. Slavery is where Black history begins. Teach them about the life long impact of slavery. Unfortunately, it is long standing. By law, US slavery ended in 1865. This belief depends on who you ask. For many, it has not ended.

W.E.B. DuBois, Frederick Douglas, Mary McLeod Bethune and others reminds us that American history has been distorted. I believe it is so important that the American history puzzle be restored to its real truth.

Additionally, many idealists believe that it is not truth per se that is important, but the search for truth. In the broadest sense, this requires passing on this knowledge and recommendations from one generation to the next, nothing less.

No, we are not responsible for the past, but we all are for the future of this country. Moreover, *we cannot continue as a divided country (S. Rice, 2020)* for our children's sake.

So, for the context of this short story narrative, a final history lesson will be given.

Actually, the 60s and 70s mirrors today's world. It is true. History does repeat itself. There were many societal problems then as now. We had a gun problem then also. President Jack Kennedy was assassinated (Nov 22, 1963). His brother, Robert Kennedy was assassinated (June 6, 1968). Martin Luther King was assassinated (April 4, 1968) right before his last speech. Malcolm X was assassinated (Feb. 21, 1965). The Viet Nam War (1955-1975) was happening, a war that society grapples with today. We were in a recession (1973-1975). Epedimics. A president some say - resigned. Others say that he was impeached in 1974.

We have the same ills as yesterday but, with a populist boldness and mostly a non-filtered technology twist. In January, a majority of the House of Representatives voted to impeach the 45th president. This was the third president to be impeached in our country. This is one year before the 2020 elections. The president continues in his position as president.

Some say, democracy is at stake (Seilfer, 2020).

There is a lot of unprecedented chaos happening in our nation, our world today.

Again, but what should Black folk be focused on while this <u>unprecedented upheaval</u> in our country unfolds? <u>We should be</u> _loving on each other. We should be STEM training our community; especially the youth. We should vote and sign up for the census._ <u>I just believe if we do, true change will come.</u>

For now, one of the best ways to show agape love is to science train our children so that they will have the digital science mindset for today's jobs thereby helping to secure their futures. This is going to require a complete change in how we treat secondary and higher education in our community.

It is time.

I say let us take this moment and clear pathways for STEM learning opportunities preventing non-traditional students from falling further behind the academic gages needed for competitive digital jobs. Who else is going to do it, if we do not pull together to start this education? Unfortunately, history and data show that our country does not "push" or "encourage" science and math instruction with any concerted holistic effort as other nations e.g., China, Singapore, Hong Kong, etc. Recent reports, schools and initiatives are beginning to emerge for the fortunate groups.

This is a national problem. It is a deep-rooted problem. History records it. For a long time, chemistry was suppressed to forms of witchcraft. When the Harvard President Eliot (1834-1926) was a student at Harvard interested in science, there were no science labs. Access to a science laboratory came through the personal friendship of a professor who at his own expense had fitted in his basement (Eliot, 1906).

Progressively during World War II (1939-1945), the nation realized that the lack of a STEM trained society was not good for the country as a whole. As stated in an earlier narrative, the government needed scientists to win the war. So, only for a while did the country make a limited science education effort [p. 42].

It was President Barack Obama and "Prez" in my book that pushed me over the hill as he and his administration recognized this US societal urgent science lack. His belief is that American children deserves access to a *"high-quality"* STEM/science education for the <u>future of the nation</u>. "Pure" science teaching has never been in effect for American Black children; never, our fault (DeNeal, 2020).

As expected of a true US leader; in his wisdom, pulled science, technology, engineering and math (STEM) experts together to research, report and show us how to address and begin to solve this national academic (both secondary and post-secondary) science problem. They recognized it.

Research does show that President Obama's administrative efforts did result in unprecedented levels of public and private policies, STEM educational plans and budgets to increase student access and engagement in active, rigorous STEM/science learning. He was concerned not only for his race, but the country as a whole. He took to heart our country's low status on the totem pole when compared to other country's science and math academic standing.

However, the president's STEM solution and budget did not reach Gary in any significant, justifiable way and we continue to drop the ball. I respect and believe in President Obama's work with this issue as I do with so many others. He fought to bring pragmatic solutions to US problems including our country's STEM/science unpreparedness while serving as president. In his own way; he has not stopped. He continues his work; especially for the young.

Unfortunately, the city of Gary secondary math and science rates remain at the lowest percentiles in the state. This is not okay. It is not.

How do we begin to change this?

First, in my community, we have science educational resources that we must continue to support with our finances, talents and volunteerism.

We have a POPS Mentoring Program headed by a Black male ER doctor that was born and raised in Gary. Our community has two government funded TRIO programs with no costs to the program participants. However, neither is a STEM project. They may offer limited science initiatives (summer camp).

Other community science and math initiatives have some costs attached except for the libraries i.e., Boys and Girls Club, YWCA, Indiana Dunes summer/winter youth science classes and weekend log cabin stays and labs for team building and science projects, Indiana University children summer science and math classes and a Purdue University Summer Youth Engineering Program.

Unfortunately, these programs are always in constant need of operating funds. Further, we have community families that cannot afford to pay for some of these activities.

Second, invest in STEM schools and initiatives and help this generation of young people move our society forward economically. This is how we move from excessive urban violence, broken families, excessive incarceration and high unemployment that has come to plague our city and so many other rural areas; one that the media needs to portray continuously, one that our children see and witness on a daily basis. How do we start?

My Dream - a STEM school on the main street of Gary, roads running from every city district and the financial and instructional strength to meet STEM learning.

Gary can run its own community STEM/science school with the approach that 1) learning and play (Froebel School of thought) and 2) science/technology ideologies are not mutually exclusive. Both, can take place at the same time to accomplish our k-12 grade science education mission and objective. **Just another reminder, our children are smart.**

This should be a STEM school where students 1-12th grades are taught science and math in every curriculum subject and matched with mentors and continuous academic remediation and interventions.

- ✓ Taught Indiana curriculums with an infused algorithm education starting in kindergarten by illustrating how cell phones and video games are designed by this type of math to **spark student's interest** in science. This can be done in a piece by piece instruction in different subjects. Be honest with the students; show them the consequences of not having this training.
- ✓ Continuous Career Training, Counseling (Mental Health); Preparation to research, write and describe annual science projects – science debate teams

- ✓ Extracurricular activities: gym, home economics, art, music, sports (swimming)
- ✓ REQUIRED READING SKILLS AND REQUIRED READING (k-12)
- ✓ Project Lead the Way software and other engineering practices beginning with grades K-3 which is the fundamental and sensory period
- ✓ Students wear assigned lab jackets to further spark their realization in these fields. Children see themselves in these careers
- ✓ Student Life - community service and afterschool initiatives, college tours, STEM clubs for competition, science/multicultural fairs
- ✓ Grades 3-6 as the skill period
- ✓ Grades 7-10 – dual credit by putting skills into practice; application for in-state college tuition
- ✓ 11th Grade as the beginning of analysis and application phase and working internships
- ✓ 12th grade as the final application theories with final demonstration of STEM science fair project. Algorithm proficiency and analysis and application for remedy for a local, state or world-wide problem with statistical results prior to enrolling in a higher education STEM degree or becoming STEM employed, published science works
- ✓ Parental Boards and Affiliations

So, how do we move on this or any other community project?

Stacy Adams (2019), offers the following recommendation and I paraphrase:

Invest in your community/claim your community-build your dream whatever it is; be innovative. You have a gift.

Talk to someone you do not know in the community

Internalize your Blackness

Be confident in who you are

Walk with your head up straight; because you know who you are

We are powerful together

We can own the Black conversation

Embrace Fear, own it, name it and make it your friend

Do Not Be Afraid of our possibilities

Innovators and Entrepreneurs Start Your Own Business – "Self-Sufficiency" – [creating, protecting and sustaining a community STEM School]

Encouraging city and secondary and post- secondary grant writing (city, state, national) to fund STEM initiatives and demanding successful school corporation including charter's proven data [70% passing state rates; particularly in science and math scores].

Most importantly, our actions will transform our communities. We can begin to fix many of our own community problems. For example, there are too many Black men walking around Gary homeless. How do you shelter in place during a pandemic when your home is on the streets?

In conclusion, as the author of this work, I just know my life experiences can help <u>inform</u> and <u>nourish</u> somebody else, especially those I love.

We have all received gifts from God. It is up to each of us to develop our gifts as best as we can for the greater good. God uses ordinary people, like me and you to contribute to His will and plan. Accept it and be the best at your God given talent.

I really do believe there is a cure for cancer, HIV, viruses and spinal cord diseases. A young mind at the proposed Gary STEM school will be educated on these possibilities. What our professionals have not discovered is discovered by our children in his or her own innovative way.

Who knows that architecture genius that is going to give the city of Gary her glory back could be growing up in our hometown as we speak just waiting for that engineering educational opportunity to come his or her way.

Another young mind may get a scientific idea while touring Gary's lakeshore historical scenes with look-a-like mentors about ways to decrease the greenhouse gases threatening our planet or assists in purported Lake County's "soil" problem and toxic dump areas that have affected our community for decades.

That little foster boy dreams of building a software that warns of world-wide disasters including global warmings while gazing out the school window at the blue sky in his 7th grade robotic engineering class.

That little immigrant African girl living in the Sanctuary City of Chicago discovers while reading the history of the 1918 Pandemic that the same preventions and cautions medical experts warned the people to use back then are the same today: <u>masking, distancing and washing of hands</u>. She became excited about her discovery. Now, her dream is to become a science writer.

I hope I live to see any of it.

I tell young people all of the time, be the expert in whatever field you are inquisitive of the most. Research and practice it over and over until you master it; no matter the circumstances. Stick with it. ***Stay focused*** and ask for help. We all did at some point in our lives.

It is worth repeating, if the politicians and leaders really want to reduce Black crime in Gary? Then, provide our young people the help they need.

Digital jobs are being created every day. So, train them for these jobs. Today, everything is moving towards some type of scientific analysis verifying such things as product validity in ways we only dream. The government sooner or later will open up infrastructure work. Will we be ready for these job opportunities? Can you imagine the types and number of job opportunities this opens up for our youth?

Should they continue to remain outside of these science opportunities when we have a chance to give them this economic power?

We have to make sure our Gary students are taught and know simple math fractions that allows community college admissions <u>before</u> they leave high school!

Thank you Amazon, UPS, McDonalds, Burger King, Wendys, Walmart, etc. for the low level *appreciated* mostly part-time job opportunities. But, we are turning this generational curse around. We want our youth trained/educated, employed with 401K retirement plans.

Timing is everything. So, hopefully, as a people, our commitment and goal going forward will be to continuously educate, train, re-educate communities of color in the occupations and work fields of STEM/science.

This education should start early in secondary school.

To be an educated person in the 21st Century is to understand something of science (Shamos, 1995).

It has been proven since the beginning, over and over again that we are a brilliant people.

Most importantly, this is another major national societal problem Black folk can overcome. We just need to *"super-serve"* the African American race! (Tom Joyner, 2019). But; as stated several times in this work, with no shift in thinking, our academic, social and economic struggle will continue or worsen.

It is a documented fact that we have failed our last two generations (especially our youth). Today, most remain out of a good education and/or a good wage resulting in a persistent poor quality of life and continual criticism by the different publics.

Let the data reflect our work:

> "Black Children have the highest math and science scores in the U.S.; especially Gary, Indiana in 2021!"

No one can argue with results.

All of this so our children can send their children, grandchildren and great grandchildren to ice lodges, summer ice skating and swimming camps, prosper, have 401Ks, live happy lives and raise families and leave inheritances for their children like everybody else.

Break the cycle!

So, I can hear my mother say right now as I bring my story to an end, "Do Not Be Afraid. Do good. Your good works will prosper wherever it goes. Just drop the seeds. God will take care of the rest.

Just Live and Serve the Lord."

I finally put the headstone on Antron's grave.

I finally put the headstone on Antron's grave.

Leaving - *My Mother's Porch.*

———∞———

Food For Thought

Our ideologies may separate us but; our pain, dreams and anger bring us all together.

So, stay in the race and Trust God

And

"Stay in Good Trouble"

– Congressman John Lewis – 2020

Just Think you're here not by chance,
but by God's choosing.
His hand formed you and
made you the person you are.
He compares you to no one else --
you are one of a kind.
You lack nothing that
His grace can't give you.
He has allowed you to
be here at this time in history
to fulfill His special purpose
for this generation.
(Roy Lessin)

So, Lord, I give you my life.
Father, I give you my gifts and talents (none that I should boast).
I give you the mess I have made of things in my life. Make
my life work meaningful and significant to your plan.

Humbly submitted,
Augusta

www.ingramcontent.com/pod-product-compliance
Lightning Source LLC
Chambersburg PA
CBHW060053100426
42742CB00014B/2801